BE SATISFIED

Be Satisfied

WARREN W. WIERSBE

While this book is intended for the reader's personal enjoyment and profit, it is also intended for group study. A leader's guide with Reproducible Response Sheets is available from your local bookstore or from the publisher.

VICTOR BOOKS ®
A DIVISION OF SCRIPTURE PRESS PUBLICATIONS INC.
USA CANADA ENGLAND

Unless otherwise noted, Scripture quotations are from the *Authorized (King James) Version.* Other quotations are from the *New American Standard Bible* (NASB), © the Lockman Foundation 1960, 1962, 1963, 1968, 1971, 1972, 1973, 1975, 1977; the *Holy Bible, New International Version* (NIV), © 1973, 1978, 1984, International Bible Society. Used by permission of Zondervan Bible Publishers; *The New Testament in Modern English,* Revised Edition, (PH), © J.B. Phillips 1958, 1960, 1972, permission of Macmillan Publishing Co. and Collins Publishers; *The New King James Version* (NKJV). © 1979, 1980, 1982, Thomas Nelson, Inc. Publishers; *The Living Bible* (TLB), © 1971, Tyndale House Publishers, Wheaton, IL 60189; and *The New English Bible,* © 1961, 1970, Oxford University Press, Cambridge University Press.

Library of Congress Cataloging-in-Publication Data

Wiersbe, Waren W.
   Be satisfied / Warren W. Wiersbe.
     p.   cm.
   ISBN 0-89693-796-8
   1. Bible. O.T. Ecclesiastes—Devotional literature.
   2. Contentment—Biblical teaching. I. Title.
   BS1475.4.W54 1990
   223'.806—dc20   89-77941
                                                  CIP

1 2 3 4 5 6 7 8 9 10 Printing/Year 94 93 92 91 90

CONTENTS

With the prayer that they will
remember their Creator in the days of their youth

This book is dedicated to our grandchildren

Jonathan
Becky, Bethany, and Daniel
Christopher and Kyle
and
Stephen

(and others that may follow)

FOREWORD

When I was asked to launch an Old Testament series of BE books, I could think of no better book to start with than Ecclesiastes. And I could think of no better title than *Be Satisfied*, because that's what Ecclesiastes is about.

"Life is filled with difficulties and perplexities," King Solomon concluded, "and there's much that nobody can understand, let alone control. From the human point of view, it's all vanity and folly. But life is God's gift to us and He wants us to enjoy it and use it for His glory. So, instead of complaining about what you don't have, start giving thanks for what you do have—and be satisfied!"

Our Jewish friends read Ecclesiastes at the annual Feast of Tabernacles, a joyful autumn festival of harvest. It fits! For Solomon wrote, "There is nothing better for a man, than that he should eat and drink, and that he should make his soul enjoy good in his labor. This also I saw, that it was from the hand of God" (Ecc. 2:24). Even the Apostle Paul (who could hardly be labeled a hedonist) said that God gives to us "richly all things to enjoy" (1 Tim. 6:17).

Life without Jesus Christ is indeed "vanity and vexation of spirit" (Ecc. 1:14). But when you know Him personally, and live for Him faithfully, you experience "fullness of joy [and] pleasures forever more" (Ps. 16:11).

Warren W. Wiersbe

ONE

Is Life Worth Living?

"Vanity of vanities," lamented Solomon, "all is vanity!" Solomon liked that word "vanity"; he used it thirty-eight times in Ecclesiastes as he wrote about life "under the sun." The word means "emptiness, futility, vapor, that which vanishes quickly and leaves nothing behind."

From the human point of view ("under the sun"), life does appear futile; and it is easy for us to get pessimistic. The Jewish writer Sholom Aleichem once described life as "a blister on top of a tumor, and a boil on top of that." You can almost *feel* that definition!

The American poet Carl Sandburg compared life to "an onion—you peel it off one layer at a time, and sometimes you weep." And British playwright George Bernard Shaw said that life was "a series of inspired follies."

When you were studying English literature in school, you may have read Matthew Arnold's poem "Rugby Chapel" in which he includes this dark description of life:

> Most men eddy about
> Here and there—eat and drink,
> Chatter and love and hate,

> Gather and squander, are raised
> Aloft, are hurl'd in the dust,
> Striving blindly, achieving
> Nothing; and then they die—

What a relief to turn from these pessimistic views and hear Jesus Christ say, "I am come that they might have life, and that they might have it more abundantly" (John 10:10). Or to read Paul's majestic declaration, "Therefore, my beloved brethren, be steadfast, unmovable, always abounding in the work of the Lord, knowing that your labor is not in vain in the Lord" (1 Cor. 15:58, NKJV).

Life is "not in vain" if it is lived according to the will of God, and that is what Solomon teaches in this neglected and often misunderstood book.

Before we embark on a study of Ecclesiastes, let's first get acquainted with the author and his aim in writing the book. We also want to get an overview of the book so we can better understand his approach to answering the question, "Is life really worth living?"

1. The Author

Nowhere in this book did the author give his name, but the descriptions he gave of himself and his experiences would indicate that the writer was King Solomon. He called himself "son of David" and "king in Jerusalem" (1:1, 12), and he claimed to have great wealth and wisdom (2:1-11, and 1:13; see 1 Kings 4:20-34 and 10:1ff). In response to Solomon's humble prayer, God promised him both wisdom and wealth (1 Kings 3:3-15); and He kept His promise.

Twelve times in Ecclesiastes the author mentioned "the king," and he made frequent references to the problems of "official bureaucracy" (4:1-3; 5:8; 8:11; 10:6-7). Keep in mind that Solomon ruled over a great nation that required a large standing army and extensive government agencies. He carried on many costly building projects and lived in luxury at court (1 Kings 9:10-28 and 10:1ff; 2 Chron. 1:13-17). Somebody had to manage all this national splendor, and somebody had to pay for it!

Solomon solved the problem by ignoring the original boundaries of the twelve tribes of Israel and dividing the nation into twelve "tax districts," each one managed by an overseer (1 Kings 4:7-19). In time, the whole system became oppressive and corrupt; and after Solomon died, the people begged for relief (2 Chron. 10). As you study Ecclesiastes, you sense this background of exploitation and oppression.

King Solomon began his reign as a humble servant of the Lord, seeking God's wisdom and help (1 Kings 3:5-15). As he grew older, his heart turned away from Jehovah to the false gods of the many wives he had taken from foreign lands (1 Kings 11:1ff). These marriages were motivated primarily by politics, not love, as Solomon sought alliances with the nations around Israel. In fact, many of the things Solomon did that seemed to bring glory to Israel were actually contrary to the Word of God (Deut. 17:14-20).

No amount of money or authority could stop the silent but sure ripening of divine judgment. The famous Scottish preacher Alexander Whyte said that "the secret worm . . . was gnawing all the time in the royal staff upon which Solomon leaned." The king's latter years were miserable because God removed His hand of blessing (1 Kings 11) and maintained Solomon's throne only because of His promise to David. After Solomon's death, the nation divided; and the house of David was left with but two tribes, Judah and Benjamin.

Ecclesiastes appears to be the kind of book a person would write near the close of life, reflecting on life's experiences and the lessons learned. Solomon probably wrote Proverbs (Prov. 1:1; 1 Kings 4:32) and the Song of Solomon (1:1) during the years he faithfully walked with God; and near the end of his life, he wrote Ecclesiastes. There is no record that King Solomon repented and turned to the Lord, but his message in Ecclesiastes suggests that he did.

He wrote Proverbs from the viewpoint of a wise teacher (1:1-6), and Song of Solomon from the viewpoint of a royal lover (3:7-11); but when he wrote Ecclesiastes, he called himself "the Preacher" (1:1, 2, 12; 7:27; 12:8-10). The Hebrew word is *Koheleth* (ko-HAY-leth) and is the title given to an official speaker who calls an assembly (see 1 Kings 8:1). The Greek word for "assembly" is *ekklesia,* and this gives us the English title of the book, Ecclesiastes.

But the Preacher did more than call an assembly and give an oration. The word Koheleth carries with it the idea of *debating,* not so much with the listeners as with himself. He would present a topic, discuss it from many viewpoints, and then come to a practical conclusion. Ecclesiastes may appear to be a random collection of miscellaneous ideas about a variety of topics, but Solomon assures us that what he wrote was orderly (12:9).

Let's consider now the aim and the development of the book.

2. The Aim

Solomon has put the key to Ecclesiastes right at the front door: "Vanity of vanities, saith the Preacher, vanity of vanities; all is vanity. What profit hath a man of all his labor which he taketh under the sun?" (1:2-3). Just in case we missed it, he put the same key at the back door (12:8). In these verses, Solomon introduces some of the key words and phrases that are used repeatedly in Ecclesiastes; so we had better get acquainted with them.

Vanity of vanities. We have already noted that Solomon used the word "vanity" thirty-eight times in this book. It is the

Hebrew word *hevel,* meaning "emptiness, futility, vapor." The name "Abel" probably comes from this word (Gen. 4:2). Whatever disappears quickly, leaves nothing behind and does not satisfy is *hevel,* vanity. One of my language professors at seminary defined *hevel* as "whatever is left after you break a soap bubble."

Whether he considers his wealth, his works, his wisdom, or his world, Solomon comes to the same sad conclusion: all is "vanity and vexation of spirit" (2:11). However, this is not his final conclusion, nor is it the only message that he has for his readers. We will discover more about that later.

Under the sun. You will find this important phrase twenty-nine times in Ecclesiastes, and with it the phrase "under heaven" (1:13; 2:3; 3:1). It defines the outlook of the writer as he looks at life from a human perspective and not necessarily from heaven's point of view. He applies his own wisdom and experience to the complex human situation and tries to make some sense out of life. Solomon wrote under the inspiration of the Holy Spirit (12:10-11; 2 Tim. 3:16), so what he wrote was what God wanted His people to have. But as we study, we must keep Solomon's viewpoint in mind: he is examining life "under the sun."

In his *Unfolding Message of the Bible,* G. Campbell Morgan perfectly summarizes Solomon's outlook: "This man had been living through all these experiences under the sun, concerned with nothing above the sun . . . until there came a moment in which he had seen the whole of life. And there was something over the sun. It is only as a man takes account of that which is over the sun as well as that which is under the sun that things under the sun are seen in their true light" (Fleming H. Revell Company, 1961, p. 229).

Profit. The Hebrew word *yitron,* usually translated "profit," is used ten times in Ecclesiastes (1:3; 2:11, 13 [excelleth]; 3:9; 5:9, 16; 7:12 [excellency]; 10:10, 11 [better]). It is used nowhere else in the Old Testament, and its basic meaning is "that which is left over." It may be translated "surplus, advantage, gain." The word "profit" is just the opposite of "vanity." Solomon asks, "In the light of all the puzzles and problems of life, what is the advantage of living? Is there any gain?"

Labor. At least eleven different Hebrew words are translated "labor" in our Authorized Version, and this one is *amal,* used twenty-three times in Ecclesiastes. It means "to toil to the point of exhaustion and yet experience little or no fulfillment in your work." It carries with it the ideas of grief, misery, frustration, and weariness. Moses expressed the meaning of this word in Deuteronomy 26:7 and Psalm 90:10. Of course, looked at only "under the sun," a person's daily work might seem to be futile and burdensome, but the Christian believer can always claim 1 Corinthians 15:58 and labor gladly in the will of God, knowing his labor is *"not* in vain in the Lord."

Man. This is the familiar Hebrew word *adam* (Genesis 1:26; 2:7, 19) and refers to man as made from the earth (*adama* in the Hebrew: Genesis 2:7; 3:19). Of course, man is made in the image of God; but he came from the earth and returns to the earth after death. Solomon used the word forty-nine times as he examined "man under the sun."

These are the basic words found in the opening verses of Ecclesiastes, but there are a few more key words that we need to consider.

Evil. This word is used thirty-one times and in the King James Version (KJV) is also translated "sore" (1:13; 4:8), "hurt" (5:13; 8:9), "mischievous" (10:13), "grievous" (2:17), "adversity" (7:14), "wickedness" (7:15), and "misery" (8:6). It is the opposite of "good" and covers a multitude of things: pain, sorrow, hard circumstances, and distress. It is one of King Solomon's favorite words for describing life as he sees it "under the sun."

Joy. In spite of his painful encounters with the world and its problems, Solomon does not recommend either pessimism or cynicism. Rather, he admonishes us to be realistic about life, accept God's gifts and enjoy them (2:24; 3:12-15, 22; 5:18-20; 8:15; 9:7-10; 11:9-10). After all, God gives to us "richly all things to enjoy" (1 Tim. 6:17). Words related to joy (enjoy, rejoice, etc.) are used at least seventeen times in Ecclesiastes. Solomon does not say, "Eat, drink, and be merry, for tomorrow you die!" Instead, he advises us to trust God and enjoy what we *do* have rather than complain about what we *don't* have. Life is short and life is difficult, so make the most of it while you can.

Wisdom. Since it is one of the Old Testament wisdom books, Ecclesiastes would have something to say about both wisdom and folly. There are at least thirty-two references to "fools" and "folly" and at least fifty-four to "wisdom." King Solomon was the wisest of men (1 Kings 4:31) and he applied this wisdom as he sought to understand the purpose of life "under the sun." The Preacher sought to be a philosopher, but in the end, he had to conclude, "Fear God, and keep His commandments" (12:13).

God. Solomon mentions God forty times and always uses "Elohim" and never "Jehovah." Elohim ("God" in the English Bible) is the Mighty God, the glorious God of creation who exercises sovereign power. Jehovah ("LORD" in the English Bible) is the God of the covenant, the God of revelation who is eternally self-existent and yet graciously relates Himself to sinful man. Since Solomon is dealing exclusively with what he sees "under the sun," he uses Elohim.

Before we leave this study of the vocabulary of Ecclesiastes, we should note that the book abounds in personal pronouns. Since it is an autobiography this is to be expected. Solomon was the ideal person to write this book, for he possessed the wealth, wisdom, and opportunities necessary to carry out the "experiments" required for this investigation into the meaning of life. God did not make King Solomon disobey just so he could write this book, but He did use Solomon's experiences to prepare him for this task.

3. The Analysis
Note the places where Solomon admonished us to enjoy life and be satisfied with what God has assigned to us.

Theme: Is life really worth living?

Key verses: 1:1-3; 12:13-14

I. THE PROBLEM DECLARED—Ecc. 1–2
Life is not worth living! Consider:
A. The monotony of life (1:4-11)
B. The vanity of wisdom (1:12-18)
C. The futility of wealth (2:1-11)
D. The certainty of death (2:12-23)
Enjoy life (2:24)

II. THE PROBLEM DISCUSSED—
Ecc. 3–10
He considers each of the above arguments:
A. The monotony of life (3:1–5:9)
1. Look up (3:1-8)
2. Look within (3:9-14)
3. Look ahead (3:15-22)
4. Look around (4:1–5:9)
Enjoy life (3:12-15, 22)
B. The futility of wealth (5:10–6:12)
1. Employing wealth (5:10-17)
2. Enjoying wealth (5:18–6:12)
Enjoy life (5:18-20)

C. The vanity of wisdom (7:1–8:17)
    1. We make life better (7:1-10)
    2. We see life clearer (7:11-18)
    3. We face life stronger (7:19–8:17)
        Enjoy life (8:15)
D. The certainty of death—(9:1–10:20)
    1. Death is unavoidable (9:1-10)
    2. Life is unpredictable (9:11-18)
    3. Beware of folly (10:1-20)
        Enjoy life (9:7-10)

III. THE PROBLEM DECIDED—Ecc. 11–12
    A. Live by faith (11:1-6)
    B. Enjoy life now (11:7–12:8)
    C. Prepare for judgment (12:9-14)
        Enjoy life (11:9-10)

In Ecclesiastes 12:8-12, Solomon explained how he wrote this book: he sought out the best words and arranged them in the best order. As he wrote, he included "goads" to prod us in our thinking and "nails" on which to hang some practical conclusions. Keep this in mind as you study. His work was inspired by God because he was guided by the "One Shepherd" (Ps. 80:1).

4. The Application
What is the practical application of this book for us today? Is Ecclesiastes nothing but an interesting exhibit in a religious museum, or does it have a message for people in the Space Age?

Its message is for today. After all, the society which Solomon investigated a millennium before the birth of Christ was not too different from our world today. Solomon saw injustice to the poor (4:1-3), crooked politics (5:8), incompetent leaders

19

(10:6-7), guilty people allowed to commit more crime (8:11), materialism (5:10), and a desire for "the good old days" (7:10). It sounds up-to-date, doesn't it?

If you have never trusted Jesus Christ as your Saviour, then this book urges you to do so without delay. Why? Because no matter how much wealth, education, or social prestige you may have, life without God is futile. You are only "chasing after the wind" if you expect to find satisfaction and personal fulfillment in the things of the world. "For what shall it profit a man, if he should gain the whole world, and lose his own soul?" asked Jesus (Mark 8:36).

Solomon experimented with life and discovered that there was no lasting satisfaction in possessions, pleasures, power, or prestige. He had everything, yet his life was empty! There is no need for you and me to repeat these experiments. Let's accept Solomon's conclusions and avoid the heartache and pain that must be endured when you experiment in the laboratory of life. These experiments are costly and one of them could prove fatal.

When you belong to the family of God through faith in the Son of God, life is not monotonous: it is a daily adventure that builds character and enables you to serve others to the glory of God. Instead of making decisions on the basis of the vain wisdom of this world, you will have God's wisdom available to you (James 1:5).

As far as wealth and pleasure are concerned, God gives to us "richly all things to enjoy" (1 Tim. 6:17). "The blessing of the Lord makes one rich, and He adds no sorrow with it" (Prov. 10:22, NKJV). The wealth and pleasures of the world do not satisfy, and the quest for power and position is futile. In Jesus Christ we have all that we need for life and death, time and eternity.

If there is one truth that Solomon emphasizes in this book, it is the certainty of death. No matter what Solomon enjoyed or accomplished, the frightening shadow of death was always hovering over him. But Jesus Christ has defeated death and is "the resurrection and the life" (John 11:25). The victory of His resurrection means that our "labor is not in vain in the Lord" (1 Cor. 15:58).

If you don't know Jesus Christ as your Saviour, then all that you work for and live for will ultimately perish; and you will perish too. But faith in Jesus Christ brings you the gift of eternal life and the privilege of serving Him and investing your years in that which is eternal.

So, the first message of Ecclesiastes is: turn from the futility of sin and the world, and put your faith in Jesus Christ (John 3:16; Eph. 2:8-10).

But if you are a believer in Jesus Christ and have received the gift of eternal life, then Solomon asks you, "Are you living for the Lord or for the things of the world?" Remember, Solomon knew God and was greatly blessed by Him, yet he turned from the Lord and went his own way. No wonder he became pessimistic and skeptical as he looked at life! He didn't have God's perspective because he wasn't living for God's purposes.

More than one professed Christian has followed Solomon's bad example and started living for the things of this world. Paul wrote about one of his associates in ministry, "Demas hath forsaken me, having loved this present world" (2 Tim. 4:10). The Apostle John warned, "Love not the world, neither the things that are in the world" (1 John 2:15); and James admonished us to keep ourselves "unspotted from the world" (1:27).

When you start living for the world instead of for the will of God, you begin to look at life from the wrong perspective: "under the sun" and not "above the sun." Instead of seeking those things which are above (Col. 3:1ff), you start majoring on the things that are below. This wrong vision soon causes you to adopt wrong values and you stop living for the eternal. The result is disappointment and defeat; the only remedy is repentance and confession of sin (1 John 1:9).

Ecclesiastes also contains a message for the faithful believer who wants to serve the Lord and have a fulfilled life in Jesus Christ. Solomon says, "Don't bury your head in the sand and pretend that problems don't exist. They do! Face life honestly, but look at life from God's perspective. Man's philosophies will fail you. Use your God-given wisdom, but don't expect to solve every problem or answer every question. The important thing is to obey God's will and enjoy all that He gives you. Remember, death is coming—so, be prepared!"

Perhaps this message is best summarized in the prayer of Moses: "So teach us to number our days, that we may apply our hearts unto wisdom" (Ps. 90:12).

I opened this chapter by quoting some metaphors that describe "life," and I want to quote one more. It's from the popular American novelist Peter De Vries: "Life is a crowded superhighway with bewildering cloverleaf exits on which a man is liable to find himself speeding back in the direction he came."

That need not happen to you! King Solomon has already explored the road exhaustively and given us a dependable map to follow. And if we follow God's Word, we will be satisfied.

Are you ready for the journey?

What will life be for you: vanity or victory?

Living in Circles

"Everything an Indian does is in a circle," said Black Elk, the Sioux religious leader. "Even the seasons form a great circle in their changing and always come back again to where they were. The life of a man is a circle from childhood to childhood. . . ."

You would think Black Elk had been studying the first chapter of Ecclesiastes, except for one fact: for centuries, wise men and women in different nations and cultures have been pondering the mysteries of the "circles" of human life. Whenever you use phrases like "life cycle," or "the wheel of fortune," or "come full circle," you are joining Solomon and Black Elk and a host of others in taking a cyclical view of life and nature.

But this "cyclical" view of life was a burden to Solomon. For if life is only part of a great cycle over which we have no control, is life worth living? If this cycle is repeated season after season, century after century, why are we unable to understand it and explain it? Solomon pondered these questions as he looked at the cycle of life "under the sun," and he came to three bleak conclusions: nothing is changed (1:4-7), nothing is new (1:8-11), and nothing is understood (1:12-18).

1. Nothing is changed (Ecc. 1:4-7)

In this section, Solomon approached the problem as a scientist and examined the "wheel of nature" around him: the earth, the sun, the wind, and the water. (This reminds us of the ancient "elements" of earth, air, fire, and water.) He was struck by the fact that generations of people came and went while the things of nature remained. There was "change" all around, yet nothing really changed. Everything was only part of the "wheel of nature" and contributed to the monotony of life. So, Solomon asked, "Is life worth living?"

Solomon presented four pieces of evidence to prove that nothing really changes.

The earth (v. 4). From the human point of view, nothing seems more permanent and durable than the planet on which we live. When we say that something is "as sure as the world," we are echoing Solomon's confidence in the permanence of planet Earth. With all of its diversity, nature is uniform enough in its operation that we can discover its "laws" and put them to work for us. In fact, it is this "dependability" that is the basis for modern science.

Nature is permanent, but man is transient, a mere pilgrim on earth. His pilgrimage is a brief one, for death finally claims him. At the very beginning of his book, Solomon introduced a topic frequently mentioned in Ecclesiastes: the brevity of life and the certainty of death.

Individuals and families come and go, nations and empires rise and fall, but nothing changes, for the world remains the same. Thomas Carlyle called history "a mighty drama, enacted upon the theater of time, with suns for lamps and eternity for a background." Solomon would add that the costumes and sets may occasionally change, but the actors and the script remain pretty much the same; and that's as sure as the world.

The sun (v. 5). We move now from the cycle of birth and death on earth to the cycle of day and night in the heavens.

24

"As sure as the world!" is replaced by "As certain as night follows day!" Solomon pictures the sun rising in the east and "panting" (literal translation) its way across the sky in pursuit of the western horizon. But what does it accomplish by this daily journey? To what purpose is all this motion and heat? As far as the heavens are concerned, one day is just like another, and the heavens remain the same.

The wind (v. 6). From the visible east-west movement of the sun, Solomon turned to the invisible north-south movement of the wind. He was not giving a lecture on the physics of wind. Rather, he was stating that the wind is in constant motion, following "circuits" that man cannot fully understand or chart. "The wind blows where it wishes," our Lord said to Nicodemus, "and you . . . cannot tell where it comes from and where it goes" (John 3:8, NKJV).

Solomon's point is this: the wind is constantly moving and changing directions, and yet it is still—the wind! We hear it and feel it, and we see what it does, but over the centuries, the wind has not changed its cycles or circuits. Man comes and goes, but the changeless wind goes on forever.

The sea (v. 7). Solomon described here the "water cycle" that helps to sustain life on our planet. Scientists tell us that, at any given time, 97 percent of all the water on earth is in the oceans; and only .0001 percent is in the atmosphere, available for rain. (That's enough for about ten days of rain.) The cooperation of the sun and the wind makes possible the evaporation and movement of moisture, and this keeps the water "circulating." But the sea never changes! The rivers and the rains pour water into the seas, but the seas remain the same.

So, whether we look at the earth or the heavens, the winds or the waters, we come to the same conclusion: nature does not change. There is motion but not *pro*motion. No wonder Solomon cites *the monotony of life* as his first argument to prove that life is not worth living (1:4-11).

All of this is true *only if you look at life "under the sun"* and leave God out of the picture. Then the world becomes a closed system that is uniform, predictable, unchangeable. It becomes a world where there are no answers to prayer and no miracles, for nothing can interrupt the cycle of nature. If there is a God in this kind of a world, He cannot act on our behalf because He is imprisoned within the "laws of nature" that cannot be suspended.

However, God *does* break into nature to do great and wonderful things! He does hear and answer prayer and work on behalf of His people. He held the sun in place so Joshua could finish an important battle (Josh. 10:6-14), and He moved the sun back as a sign to King Hezekiah (Isa. 38:1-8). He opened the Red Sea and the Jordan River for Israel (Ex. 14; Josh. 3–4). He "turned off" the rain for Elijah (1 Kings 17) and then "turned it on" again (James 5:17-18). He calmed the wind and the waves for the disciples (Mark 4:35-41), and in the future, will use the forces of nature to bring terror and judgment to people on the earth (see Revelation 6ff).

When, by faith, you receive Jesus Christ as your Saviour, and God becomes your Heavenly Father, you no longer live in a "closed system" of endless monotonous cycles. You can gladly sing, "This is my Father's world!" and know that He will meet your every need as you trust Him (Matt. 6:25-34). Christians live in this world as pilgrims, not prisoners, and therefore they are joyful and confident.

2. Nothing is new (Ecc. 1:8-11)

If nothing changes, then it is reasonable to conclude that nothing in this world is new. This "logical conclusion" might have satisfied people in Solomon's day, but it startles us today. After all, we are surrounded by, and dependent on, a multitude of marvels that modern science has provided for us—everything from telephones to pacemakers and miracle drugs.

How could anybody who watched Neil Armstrong walk on the moon agree with Solomon that nothing is new under the sun?

In this discussion, Solomon stopped being a scientist and became a historian. Let's follow the steps in his reasoning.

Man wants something new (v. 8). Why? Because everything in this world ultimately brings weariness, and people long for something to distract them or deliver them. They are like the Athenians in Paul's day, spending their time "in nothing else, but either to tell, or to hear some new thing" (Acts 17:21). But even while they are speaking, seeing, and hearing these "new things," they are still dissatisfied with life and will do almost anything to find some escape. Of course, the entertainment industry is grateful for this human hunger for novelty and takes advantage of it at great profit.

In Ecclesiastes 3:11, Solomon explains why men and women are not satisfied with life: God has put "eternity in their heart" (NIV, NASB, NKJV) and nobody can find peace and satisfaction apart from Him. "Thou hast made us for Thyself," prayed St. Augustine, "and our hearts are restless until they rest in Thee." The eye cannot be satisfied until it sees the hand of God, and the ear cannot be satisfied until it hears the voice of God. We must respond by faith to our Lord's invitation, "Come unto me . . . and I will give you rest" (Matt. 11:28).

The world provides nothing new (vv. 9-10). Dr. H.A. Ironside, longtime pastor of Chicago's Moody church, used to say, "If it's new, it's not true; and if it's true, it's not new." Whatever is new is simply a recombination of the old. Man cannot "create" anything new because man is the creature, not the Creator. "That which hath been is now, and that which is to be hath already been" (3:15). Thomas Alva Edison, one of the world's greatest inventors, said that his inventions were only "bringing out the secrets of nature and applying them for the happiness of mankind."

Only God can create new things, and he begins by making

sinners "new creatures" when they trust Jesus Christ to save them (2 Cor. 5:17). Then they can walk "in newness of life" (Rom. 6:4), sing a "new song" (Ps. 40:3), and enter into God's presence by a "new and living way" (Heb. 10:20). One day, they will enjoy "a new heaven and a new earth" (Rev. 21:1) when God says, "Behold, I make all things new" (Rev. 21:5).

Why we think things are new (v. 11). The answer is simple: we have bad memories and we don't read the minutes of the previous meeting. (See 2:16, 4:16, and 9:5.) It has well been said that the ancients have stolen all of our best ideas, and this is painfully true.

A young man approached me at a conference and asked if he could share some new ideas for youth ministry. He was very enthusiastic as he outlined his program; but the longer I listened, the more familiar his ideas became. I encouraged him to put his ideas into practice, but then told him that we had done all of those things in Youth for Christ before he was born, and that YFC workers were still doing them. He was a bit stunned to discover that there was indeed nothing new under the sun.

Solomon wrote, of course, about the basic principles of life and not about methods. As the familiar couplet puts it: Methods are many, principles are few / methods always change, principles never do. The ancient thinkers knew this. The Stoic philosopher Marcus Aurelius wrote, "They that come after us will see nothing new, and they who went before us saw nothing more than we have seen." The only people who really think they have seen something new are those whose experience is limited or whose vision can't penetrate beneath the surface of things. Because something is recent, they think it is new; they mistake novelty for originality.

3. Nothing is understood (Ecc. 1:12-18)

The historian now becomes the philosopher as Solomon tells how he went about searching for the answer to the problem that vexed him. As the king of Israel, he had all the resources necessary for "experimenting" with different solutions to see what it was that made life worth living. In the laboratory of life, he experimented with enjoying various physical pleasures (2:1-3), accomplishing great and costly works (2:4-6), and accumulating great possessions (2:7-10) only to discover that all of it was only "vanity and grasping for the wind" (v. 14, NKJV).

But before launching into his experiments, Solomon took time to try to think the matter through. He was the wisest of all men and he applied that God-given wisdom to the problem. He devoted his mind wholly to the matter to get to the root of it ("seek") and to explore it from all sides ("search"). Dorothy Sayers wrote in one of her mystery novels, "There is nothing you cannot prove if only your outlook is narrow enough." Solomon did not take that approach.

Here are some of his tentative conclusions:

Life is tough, but it is the gift of God (v. 13). He described life as a "sore travail" ("grievous task," NKJV) that only fatigues you ("may be exercised", NKJV). Of course, when God first gave life to man, the world had not been cursed because of sin (Gen. 3:14ff). Since the Fall of man, "the whole creation groans and labors with birth pangs" (Rom. 8:22, NKJV); this is one reason why life is so difficult. One day, when our Lord returns, creation will be delivered from this bondage.

While sitting in my backyard one evening, I heard a robin singing merrily from atop a TV aerial. As I listened to him sing, I preached myself a sermon:

> Since early dawn, that bird has done nothing but try to survive. He's been wearing himself out hiding from enemies and looking for food for himself and his little ones. And yet, when he gets to the end of the day, *he sings about it!*

Here I am, created in the image of God and saved by

the grace of God, and I complain about even the little annoyances of life. One day, I will be like the Lord Jesus Christ; for that reason alone, I should be singing God's praises just like that robin.

Life doesn't get easier if you try to run away from it (v. 14). All the works that are done "under the sun" never truly satisfy the heart. They are but "vanity and grasping for the wind" (v. 14, NKJV). Both the workaholic and the alcoholic are running away from reality and living on substitutes, and one day the bubble of illusion will burst. We only make life harder when we try to escape. Instead of running away from life, we should run to God and let Him make life worth living.

The ultimate door of escape is suicide, and Solomon will have something to say about man's desire for death. Some specialists claim that 40,000 persons commit suicide in the United States annually, and an estimated 400,000 make the attempt. But once you have *chosen to live* and have rightly rejected suicide as an option, then you must choose *how* you are going to live. Will it be by faith in yourself and what you can do, or by faith in the Lord?

Not everything can be changed (v. 15). It is likely that Solomon, who was an expert on proverbs (1 Kings 4:32), quoted a popular saying here in order to make his point. He makes a similar statement in 7:13. If we spend all our time and energy trying to straighten out everything that is twisted, we will have nothing left with which to live our lives! And if we try to spend what we don't have, we will end up in bankruptcy.

In short, Solomon is saying, "The past can't always be changed, and it is foolish to fret over what you might have done." Ken Taylor paraphrases verse 15, "What is wrong cannot be righted; it is water over the dam; and there is no use thinking of what might have been" (TLB).

We must remind ourselves, however, that God has the

power to straighten out what is twisted and supply what is lacking. He cannot change the past, but He can change the way that the past affects us. For the lost sinner, the past is a heavy anchor that drags him down; but for the child of God, the past—even with its sins and mistakes—is a rudder that guides him forward. Faith makes the difference.

When He was ministering here on earth, our Lord often straightened out that which was twisted and provided that which was lacking (Luke 13:11-17; Matt. 12:10-13, 15:29-39; John 6:1-13). Man cannot do this by his own wisdom or power, but "with God nothing shall be impossible" (Luke 1:37). Solomon was looking at these problems from a vantage point "under the sun," and that's why they seemed insoluble.

Wisdom and experience will not solve every problem (vv. 16-18). Those who go through life living on explanations will always be unhappy for at least two reason. First, this side of heaven, there are no explanations for some things that happen, and God is not obligated to explain them anyway. (In fact, if He did, we might not understand them!) Second, God has ordained that His people live by *promises* and not by explanations, by faith and not by sight. "Blessed are they that have not seen, and yet have believed" (John 20:29).

If anybody was equipped to solve the difficult problems of life and tell us what life was all about, Solomon was that person. He was the wisest of men, and people came from all over to hear his wisdom (1 Kings 4:29-34). His wealth was beyond calculation so that he had the resources available to do just about anything he wanted to do. He even experienced "madness and folly" (the absurd, the opposite of wisdom) in his quest for the right answers. Nothing was too hard for him.

But these advantages didn't enable Solomon to find all the answers he was seeking. In fact, his great wisdom only *added* to his difficulties; for wisdom and knowledge increase sorrow and grief. People who never ponder the problems of life, who live innocently day after day, never feel the pain of wrestling with God in seeking to understand His ways. The more we seek knowledge and wisdom, the more ignorant we know we are. This only adds to the burden. "All our knowledge brings us nearer to our ignorance," wrote T.S. Eliot in "Choruses From 'The Rock.'" An old proverb says, "A wise man is never happy."

All of this goes back to the Garden of Eden and Satan's offer to Eve that, if she ate of the fruit, she would have the knowledge of good and evil (Gen. 3). When Adam and Eve sinned, they did get an experiential knowledge of good and evil; but, since they were alienated from God, this knowledge only *added* to their sorrows. It has been that way with man ever since. Whether it be jet planes, insecticides, or television, each advance in human knowledge and achievement only creates a new set of problems for society.

For some people, life may be monotonous and meaningless; but it doesn't have to be. For the Christian believer, life is an open door, not a closed circle; there are daily experiences of new blessings from the Lord. True, we can't explain everything; but life is not built on explanations: it's built on promises—and we have plenty of promises in God's Word!

The scientist tells us that the world is a closed system and nothing is changed.

The historian tells us that life is a closed book and nothing is new.

The philosopher tells us that life is a deep problem and nothing is understood.

But Jesus Christ is "the power of God and the wisdom of God" (1 Cor. 1:24), and He has miraculously broken into history to bring new life to all who trust Him.

If you are "living in circles," then turn your life over to Him.

Disgusted with Life?

There is but one step from the sublime to the ridiculous."
Napoleon is supposed to have made that statement after
his humiliating retreat from Moscow in the winter of 1812.
The combination of stubborn Russian resistance and a severe
Russian winter was too much for the French army, and its
expected sublime victory was turned into shameful defeat.

As part of his quest for "the good life," King Solomon examined everything from the sublime to the ridiculous. In the great
laboratory of life, he experimented with one thing after another, always applying the wisdom that God had given him (vv. 3,
9). In this chapter, Solomon recorded three stages in his experiments as he searched for a satisfying meaning to life.

1. He tested life (Ecc. 2:1-11)

Solomon had the means and the authority to do just about
anything his heart desired. He decided to test his own heart to
see how he would respond to two very common experiences
of life: enjoyment (1-3) and employment (4-11).

Enjoyment (2:1-3). The Hebrew people rightly believed that
God made man to enjoy the blessings of His creation (Ps. 104,
and note 1 Tim. 6:17). The harvest season was a joyful time

33

for them as they reaped the blessings of God on their labor. At the conclusion of his book, Solomon admonished his readers to enjoy God's blessings during the years of their youth, before old age arrived and the body began to fall apart (12:1ff). Eight times in Ecclesiastes, Solomon used the Hebrew word meaning "pleasure," so it is obvious that he did not consider God a celestial spoilsport who watched closely to make certain nobody was having a good time.

Solomon specifically mentioned wine and laughter as two sources of pleasure used in his experiment. It takes very little imagination to see the king in his splendid banquet hall (1 Kings 10:21), eating choice food (1 Kings 4:22-23), drinking the very best wine, and watching the most gifted entertainers (2:8b). But when the party was over and King Solomon examined his heart, it was still dissatisfied and empty. Pleasure and mirth were only vanity, so many soap bubbles that quickly burst and left nothing behind.

Perhaps many of the king's servants envied Solomon and wished to change places with him, but the king was unhappy. "Even in laughter the heart is sorrowful," he wrote in Proverbs 14:13, "and the end of that mirth is heaviness."

Today's world is pleasure-mad. Millions of people will pay almost any amount of money to "buy experiences" and temporarily escape the burdens of life. While there is nothing wrong with innocent fun, the person who builds his or her life only on seeking pleasure is bound to be disappointed in the end.

Why? For one thing, pleasure-seeking usually becomes a selfish endeavor; and selfishness destroys true joy. People who live for pleasure often exploit others to get what they want, and they end up with broken relationships as well as empty hearts. *People are more important than things and thrills.* We are to be channels, not reservoirs; the greatest joy comes when we share God's pleasures with others.

If you live for pleasure alone, enjoyment will decrease unless the intensity of the pleasure increases. Then you reach a point of diminishing returns when there is little or no enjoyment at all, only bondage. For example, the more that people drink, the less enjoyment they get out of it. This means they must have more drinks and stronger drinks in order to have pleasure; the sad result is desire without satisfaction. Instead of alcohol, substitute drugs, gambling, sex, money, fame, or any other pursuit, and the principle will hold true: when pleasure alone is the center of life, the result will ultimately be disappointment and emptiness.

There is a third reason why pleasure alone can never bring satisfaction: it appeals to only part of the person and ignores the total being. This is the major difference between shallow "entertainment" and true "enjoyment," for when the whole person is involved, there will be both enjoyment and enrichment. Entertainment has its place, but we must keep in mind that it only helps us to escape life temporarily. True pleasure not only brings delight, but it also builds character by enriching the total person.

Employment (2:4-11). Next, Solomon got involved in all kinds of projects, hoping to discover something that would make life worth living. He started with *great works* (4-6), including houses (1 Kings 7), cities (2 Chron. 8:4-6), gardens, vineyards, orchards and forests (1 Kings 4:33), and the water systems needed to service them. Of course, Solomon also supervised the construction of the temple (1 Kings 5ff), one of the greatest buildings of the ancient world.

He not only had works, but he also had *workers* (7a). He had two kinds of slaves: those he purchased and those born in his household. He might have added that he "drafted" 30,000 Jewish men to work on various projects (1 Kings 5:13-18). His father David had conscripted the strangers in the land (1 Chron. 22:2), but Solomon drafted his own people, and the people resented it (see 1 Kings 12).

Of course, Solomon accumulated *wealth* (7b-8a), in flocks and herds (1 Kings 8:63) as well as gold and silver (1 Kings 4:21 and 10:1ff). He was the wealthiest and wisest man in the whole world, yet he was unhappy because activity alone does not bring lasting pleasure.

There can be joy in the *doing* of great projects, but what happens when the task is finished? Solomon found delight *in* all his labor (2:10); but *afterward,* when he considered all his works, he saw only "vanity and vexation of spirit" (2:11). The journey was a pleasure, but the destination brought pain. "Success is full of promise until men get it," said the American preacher Henry Ward Beecher, "and then it is a last-year's nest from which the birds have flown."

We must not conclude that Solomon was condemning work itself, because work is a blessing from God. Adam had work to do in the Garden even before he sinned. "The Lord God took the man and put him in the Garden of Eden to work it and take care of it" (Gen. 2:15, NIV). In the Book of Proverbs, Solomon exalted diligence and condemned laziness; for he knew that any honest employment can be done to the glory of God (1 Cor. 10:31). But work *alone* cannot satisfy the human heart, no matter how successful that work may be (Isa. 55:2).

This helps us to understand why many achievers are unhappy people. Ambrose Bierce called achievement "the death of endeavor and the birth of disgust." This is often the case. The overachiever is often a person who is trying to escape himself or herself by becoming a workaholic, and this only results in disappointment. When workaholics retire, they often feel useless and sometimes die from lack of meaningful activity.

Solomon tested life, and his heart said, "Vanity!"

2. Solomon hated life (Ecc. 2:12-23)

"I turned myself to behold" simply means, "I considered things from another viewpoint." What he did was to look at his wisdom (12-17) and his wealth (18-23) *in light of the certainty of death.* What good is it to be wise and wealthy if you are going to die and leave everything behind?

The certainty of death is a topic Solomon frequently mentioned in Ecclesiastes (1:4; 2:14-17; 3:18-20; 5:15-16; 6:6; 8:8; 9:2-3, 12; 12:7-8). He could not easily avoid the subject as he looked at life "under the sun," for death is one of the obvious facts of life. The French essayist Montaigne wrote, "Philosophy is no other thing than for a man to prepare himself to death." Only that person is prepared to live who is prepared to die.

He considered his wisdom (2:12-17). Since both the wise man and the fool will die, what is the value of wisdom? For one thing, we can leave our wisdom for the guidance of the next generation; but how can we be sure they will value it or follow it? "What can the man do that cometh after the king?" suggests that it is folly for successive generations to make the same "experiments" (and mistakes) when they can learn from their forefathers; *but they do it just the same!* There is nothing new under the sun (1:9); they can only repeat what we have already done.

In spite of the fact that all men must die, wisdom is still of greater value than folly. They are as different as night and day! *The wise man sees that death is coming and lives accordingly, while the fool walks in darkness and is caught unprepared.* However, being prepared for death does not necessarily relieve Solomon of his burden about life; for it takes a person a long time to learn how to live, and then life ends. All of this seems so futile.

Both the wise man and the fool die, and both the wise man and the fool are forgotten (v. 16). Solomon's fame has remained, of course (1 Kings 4:29-34; Matt. 6:28-30); but most "famous" people who have died are rarely mentioned in ordinary conversation, although their biographies are found in the encyclopedias. (I note that some of these biographies get smaller from edition to edition.)

"So I hated life!" concluded Solomon, but he was not contemplating suicide; for death was one thing he wanted to avoid. "I hate life and yet I am afraid to die!" said the French humanist Voltaire; Solomon would agree with him. Life seemed irrational and futile to Solomon, and yet it was still better than death. We might paraphrase his statement, "Therefore, I was disgusted with life!"

The healthy Christian believer certainly would not hate life, no matter how difficult the circumstances might be. It is true that some great men have wanted to die, such as Job (Job 3:21–7:15), Moses (Num. 11:15), Elijah (1 Kings 19:4), and Jonah (Jonah 4:3), but we must not take these special instances as examples for us to follow. All of these men finally changed their minds.

No, the Christian should "love life" (1 Peter 3:10, quoted from Ps. 34:12ff), seeking to put the most into it and getting the most out of it, to the glory of God. We may not enjoy everything in life, or be able to explain everything about life, but that is not important. We live by promises and not by explanations, and we know that our "labor is not in vain in the Lord" (1 Cor. 15:58).

He considered his wealth (2:18-23). Not only did Solomon hate life, but he hated the wealth that was the result of his toil. Of course, Solomon was born wealthy, and great wealth came to him because he was the king. But he was looking at life "under the sun" and speaking for the "common people" who were listening to his discussion. He gave three reasons why he was disgusted with wealth.

First, *you can't keep it* (v. 18). The day would come when Solomon would die and leave everything to his successor. This reminds us of our Lord's warning in the Parable of the Rich Fool (Luke 12:13-21) and Paul's words in 1 Timothy 6:7-10. A

38

Jewish proverb says, "There are no pockets in shrouds."

Money is a medium of exchange. Unless it is spent, it can do little or nothing for you. You can't eat money, but you can use it to buy food. It will not keep you warm, but it will purchase fuel. A writer in *The Wall Street Journal* called money "an article which may be used as a universal passport to everywhere except heaven, and as a universal provider of everything except happiness."

Of course, you and I are *stewards* of our wealth; God is the Provider (Deut. 8:18) and the Owner, and we have the privilege of enjoying it and using it for His glory. One day we will have to give an account of what we have done with His generous gifts. While we cannot take wealth with us when we die, we can "send it ahead" as we use it today according to God's will (Matt. 6:19-34).

Second, *we can't protect it* (vv. 19-20). It's bad enough that we must leave our wealth behind, but even worse that we might leave it to somebody who will waste it! Suppose he or she is a fool and tears down everything we have built up? Solomon didn't know it at the time, but his son Rehoboam would do that very thing (1 Kings 11:41–12:24).

Many people have tried to write their wills in such a way that their estates could not be wasted, but they have not always succeeded. In spite of the instruction and good example they may give, the fathers and mothers have no way of knowing what the next generation will do with the wealth that they worked so hard to accumulate. Solomon's response was to walk about and simply resign himself ("despair" v. 20) to the facts of life and death. As the rustic preacher said, "We all must learn to cooperate with the inevitable!"

Third, *we can't enjoy it as we should* (vv. 21-23). If all we do is think about our wealth and worry about what will happen to it, we will make our lives miserable. We do all the work and then leave the wealth to somebody who didn't even work for it

(v. 21). Is that fair? We spend days in travail and grief and have many sleepless nights, yet our heirs never experience any of this . It all seems so futile. "What does a man get for all the toil and anxious striving with which he labors under the sun?" (v. 22, NIV)

At this point, Solomon appears to be very pessimistic, but he doesn't remain that way very long. In a step of faith he reaches the third stage in his experiment.

3. He accepted life (2:24-26)

This is the first of six "conclusions" in Ecclesiastes, each of which emphasizes the importance of accepting life as God's gift and enjoying it in God's will (3:12-15, 22; 5:18-20; 8:15; 9:7-10; 11:9-10). Solomon is not advocating "Eat, drink and be merry, for tomorrow we die!" That is the philosophy of fatalism not faith. Rather, he is saying, "Thank God for what you do have, and enjoy it to the glory of God." Paul gave his approval to this attitude when he exhorted us to trust "in the living God, who gives us richly all things to enjoy" (1 Tim. 6:17, NKJV).

Solomon made it clear that not only were the blessings from God, but even the *enjoyment of the blessings* was God's gift to us (v. 24). He considered it "evil" if a person had all the blessings of life from God but could not enjoy them (6:1-5). It is easy to see why the Jewish people read Ecclesiastes at the Feast of Tabernacles, for Tabernacles is their great time of thanksgiving and rejoicing for God's abundant provision of their needs.

The translation of v. 25 in the King James Version is somewhat awkward; the New American Standard Bible is better: "For who can eat and who can have enjoyment without Him?" The farmer who prayed at the table, "Thanks for food and for good digestion" knew what Solomon was writing about.

The important thing is that we seek to please the Lord

(v. 26) and trust Him to meet every need. God wants to give us wisdom, knowledge, and joy; these three gifts enable us to appreciate God's blessings and take pleasure in them. *It is not enough to possess "things"; we must also possess the kind of character that enables us to use "things" wisely and enjoy them properly.*

Not so with the sinner. (The Hebrew word means "to fall short, to miss the mark.") The sinner may heap up all kinds of riches, but he can never truly enjoy them because he has left God out of his life. In fact, his riches may finally end up going to the righteous. This is not always the case, but God does make it happen that "the wealth of the sinner is laid up for the just" (Prov. 13:22). At their exodus from Egypt, the Israelites spoiled their Egyptian masters (Ex. 3:22; 12:36), and throughout Jewish history their armies took great spoil in their many conquests. In fact, much of the wealth that went into the temple came from David's military exploits.

It is "vanity and vexation of spirit" ("meaningless, a chasing after wind," NIV) for the sinner to heap up riches and yet ignore God. Apart from God, there can be no true enjoyment of blessings or enrichment of life. It is good to have the things that money can buy, *provided* you don't lose the things that money can't buy.

This completes the first section of Ecclesiastes—*The Problem Declared.* Solomon has presented four arguments that seem to prove that life is really not worth living: the monotony of life (1:4-11), the vanity of wisdom (1:12-18), the futility of wealth (2:1-11), and the certainty of death (2:12-23). His argument appears to be true *if* you look at life "under the sun," that is, only from the human point of view.

But when you bring God into the picture, everything changes! (Note that God is not mentioned from 1:14 to 2:23.) Life and death, wisdom and wealth, are all in His hands; He wants us to enjoy His blessings and please His heart. If we rejoice in the gifts, but forget the Giver, then we are ungrateful idolaters.

In the next eight chapters, Solomon will consider each of these four arguments and refute them. At the end of each argument he will say, "Enjoy life and be thankful to God!" (See the outline on pages 18–19.) In his discussions, he will face honestly the trials and injustices of life, the things that make us cry out, "Why, Lord?" But Solomon is not a shallow optimist wearing rose-tinted glasses, nor is he a skeptical pessimist wearing blinders. Rather, he takes a balanced view of life and death and helps us look at both from God's eternal perspective.

"Life isn't like a book," says Chuck Colson, founder of Prison Fellowship ministry. "Life isn't logical, or sensible, or orderly. Life is a mess most of the time. And theology must be lived in the midst of that mess."

Solomon will provide us with that theology.

It's up to us to live it—and *be satisfied!*

FOUR

ECCLESIASTES 3

Time and Toil

Ponder these quotations from two famous professors: "Why shouldn't things be largely absurd, futile, and transitory? They are so, and we are so, and they and we go very well together." That's from philosopher George Santayana, who taught at Harvard from 1889 to 1912.

"There is no reason to suppose that a man's life has any more meaning than the life of the humblest insect that crawls from one annihilation to another." That was written by Joseph Wood Krutch, professor of English at Columbia University from 1937 to 1952.

Both of these men were brilliant in their fields, but most of us would not agree with what they wrote. We believe that something grander is involved in human life than mere transitory existence. We are *not* like insects. Surely Dr. Krutch knew that insects have *life cycles,* but men and women have *histories.* One bee is pretty much like another bee, but people are unique and no two stories are the same. You can write *The Life of the Bee,* but you can't write *The Life of the Man* or *The Life of the Woman.*

If we as individuals are not unique, then we are not important; if we are not important, then life has no meaning. If life has no meaning, life isn't worth living. We might as well follow the Epicurean philosophy: "Let us eat and drink, for tomorrow we die."

Solomon has presented four arguments proving that life was nothing but grasping broken soap bubbles and chasing after the wind. But he was too wise a man to let his own arguments go unchallenged, so in Ecclesiastes 3–10, he reexamined each of them carefully. His first argument was *the monotony of life* (1:4-11), and he examined it in Ecclesiastes 3:1–5:9. He discovered four factors that must be considered before you can say that life is monotonous and meaningless.

First, he saw something *above* man, a God who was in control of time and who balanced life's experiences (3:1-8). Then he saw something *within* man that linked him to God—eternity in his heart (3:9-14). Third, Solomon saw something *ahead of* man—the certainty of death (3:15-22). Finally, he saw something *around* man—the problems and burdens of life (4:1–5:9).

So, The Preacher asked his listeners to look up, to look within, to look ahead, and to look around, and to take into consideration time, eternity, death, and suffering. These are the four factors God uses to keep our lives from becoming monotonous and meaningless. We will consider three of these factors in this chapter and the fourth in our next study.

1. Look up: God orders time (Ecc. 3:1-8)

You don't have to be a philosopher or a scientist to know that "times and seasons" are a regular part of life, no matter where you live. Were it not for the dependability of God-ordained "natural laws," both science and daily life would be chaotic, if not impossible. Not only are there times and seasons in this world, but there is also an overruling providence in our lives. From before our birth to the moment of our death, God is accomplishing His divine purposes, even though we may not always understand what He is doing.

In fourteen statements, Solomon affirmed that God is at work in our individual lives, seeking to accomplish His will. All of these events come from God and they are good *in their time*. The inference is plain: if we cooperate with God's timing, life will not be meaningless. Everything will be "beautiful in His time" (v. 11), even the most difficult experiences of life. Most of these statements are easy to understand, so we will examine only those that may need special explanation.

Birth and death (v. 2). Things like abortion, birth control, mercy killing, and surrogate parenthood make it look as though man is in control of birth and death, but Solomon said otherwise. Birth and death are not human accidents; they are divine appointments, for God is in control. (Read Gen. 29:31–30:24 and 33:5; Josh. 24:3; 1 Sam. 1:9-20; Pss. 113:9 and 127; Jer. 1:4-5; Luke 1:5-25; Gal. 1:15 and 4:4.) Psalm 139:13-16 states that God so wove us in the womb that our genetic structure is perfect for the work He has prepared for us to do (Eph. 2:10). We may foolishly hasten our death, but we cannot prevent it when our time comes, unless God so wills it (Isa. 38). "All the days ordained for me were written in Your book" (Ps. 139:16, NIV).

Planting and plucking (v. 2). Being an agricultural people, the Jews appreciated the seasons. In fact, their religious calendar was based on the agricultural year (Lev. 23). Men may plow and sow, but only God can give the increase (Ps. 65:9-13). "Plucking" may refer either to reaping or to pulling up unproductive plants. A successful farmer knows that nature works for him only if he works with nature. This is also the secret of a successful life: learn God's principles and cooperate with them.

Killing and healing (v. 3). This probably refers, not to war (v. 8) or self-defense, but to the results of sickness and plague in the land (1 Sam. 2:6). God permits some to die while others are healed. This does not imply that we should refuse medical aid, for God can use both means and miracles to accomplish His purposes (Isa. 38).

Casting away stones and gathering stones (v. 5). Tour guides in Israel will tell you that God gave stones to an angel and told him to distribute them across the world—and he tripped right over Palestine! It is indeed a rocky land and farmers must clear their fields before they can plow and plant. If you wanted to hurt an enemy, you filled up his field with stones (2 Kings 3:19, 25). People also gathered stones for building walls and houses. Stones are neither good nor bad; it all depends on what you do with them. If your enemy fills your land with rocks, don't throw them back. Build something out of them!

Embracing and refraining from embracing (v. 5). People in the Near East openly show their affections, kissing and hugging when they meet and when they part. So, you could paraphrase this, "A time to say hello and a time to say good-bye." This might also refer to the relationship of a husband and wife (Lev. 15:19-31; and see 1 Cor. 7:5).

Getting and losing (v. 6). "A time to search and a time to give it up for lost" is another translation. The next phrase gives biblical authority for garage sales: a time to keep and a time to clean house!

Tearing and mending (v. 7). This probably refers to the Jewish practice of tearing one's garments during a time of grief or repentance (2 Sam. 13:31; Ezra 9:5). God expects us to sorrow during bereavement, but not like unbelievers (1 Thes. 4:13-18). There comes a time when we must get out the needle and thread and start sewing things up!

Loving and hating (v. 8). Are God's people allowed to hate? The fact that the next phrase mentions "war and peace" suggests that Solomon may have had the nation primarily in mind. However, there are some things that even Christians ought to hate (2 Chron. 19:2; Ps. 97:10; Prov. 6:16-19; Rev. 2:6, 15).

Life is something like a doctor's prescription: taken alone, the ingredients might kill you; but properly blended, they bring healing. God is sovereignly in control and has a time and a purpose for everything (Rom. 8:28). This is not fatalism, nor does it rob us of freedom or responsibility. It is the wise providence of a loving Father Who does all things well and promises to make everything work for good.

2. Look within: eternity is in your heart (Ecc. 3:9-14)
The Preacher adjusted his sights and no longer looked at life *only* "under the sun." He brought God into the picture and this gave him a new perspective. In verse 9, he repeated the opening question of 1:3, "Is all this labor really worth it?" In the light of "new evidence," Solomon gave three answers to the question.

First, *man's life is a gift from God* (v. 10). In view of the travail that we experience from day to day, life may seem like a strange gift, but it is God's gift just the same. We "exercise" ourselves in trying to explain life's enigmas, but we don't always succeed. If we believingly accept life as a gift, and thank God for it, we will have a better attitude toward the burdens that come our way. If we grudgingly accept life as a burden, then we will miss the gifts that come our way. Outlook helps to determine outcome.

Second, *man's life is linked to eternity.* (v. 11). Man was created in the image of God, and was given dominion over creation (Gen. 1:26-28); therefore, he is different from the rest of creation. He has "eternity ["the world," KJV] in his heart" and is linked to heaven. This explains why nobody (including Solomon) can be satisfied with his or her endeavors and achievements, or is able to explain the enigmas of life (1:12–2:11). God accomplishes His purposes in His time, but it will not be until we enter eternity that we will begin to comprehend His total plan.

Third, *man's life can be enjoyable now* (vv. 12-14). The Preacher hinted at this in 2:24 and was careful to say that this enjoyment of life is the gift of God (see 3:13, 6:2, and 1 Tim. 6:17). "The enjoyment of life" is an important theme in Ecclesiastes and is mentioned in each of the four sections of chapters 3–10. (Review the outline on pages 18–19.) Solomon is encouraging not pagan hedonism, but rather the practice of enjoying God's gifts as the fruit of one's labor, no matter how difficult life may be. Life appears to be transitory, but whatever God does is forever, so when we live for Him and let Him have His way, life is meaningful and manageable. Instead of complaining about what we don't have, let's enjoy what we do have and thank God for it.

When the well-known British Methodist preacher William Sangster learned that he had progressive muscular atrophy and could not get well, he made four resolutions and kept them to the end: (1) I will never complain; (2) I will keep the home bright; (3) I will count my blessings; (4) I will try to turn it to gain. This is the approach to life that Solomon wants us to take.

However, we must note that Solomon is not saying, "Don't worry—be happy!" He is promoting faith in God, not "faith in faith" or "pie in the sky by and by." Faith is only as good as the *object* of faith, and the greatest object of faith is the Lord. He can be trusted.

How can life be meaningless and monotonous for you when God has made you a part of His eternal plan? You are not an insignificant insect, crawling from one sad annihilation to another. If you have trusted Jesus Christ, you are a child of God being prepared for an eternal home (John 14:1-6; 2 Cor. 4). The Puritan pastor Thomas Watson said, "Eternity to the godly is a day that has no sunset; eternity to the wicked is a night that has no sunrise."

The proper attitude for us is the fear of the Lord (v. 14),

which is not the cringing of a slave before a cruel master, but the submission of an obedient child to a loving parent. (See 5:7, 7:18, 8:12-13, and 12:13.) If we fear God, we need not fear anything else for He is in control.

3. Look ahead: death is coming to all (Ecc. 3:15-22)

Solomon already mentioned the certainty of death in 2:12-23, and he will bring the subject up several times before he ends his book (4:8; 5:15-16; 6:6; 8:8; 9:2-3, 12; 12:7-8). Life, death, time, and eternity: these are the "ingredients" that make up our brief experience in this world, and they must not be ignored.

Verse 15 helps us recall 1:9-11 and gives us the assurance that God is in control of the "cycle of life." The past seems to repeat itself so that "there is no new thing under the sun" (1:9), but God can break into history and do what He pleases. His many miracles are evidence that the "cycle" is a pattern and not a prison. His own Son broke into human life through a miraculous birth. He then died on a cross and rose again, thus conquering the "life-death cycle." Because Jesus Christ broke the "vicious circle," He can make us a part of a new creation that overcomes time and death (2 Cor. 5:17-21).

Solomon added a new thought here: "and God will call the past to account" (v. 15, NIV). Scholars have a difficult time agreeing on the translation of this phrase. It literally says "God seeks what hurries along." Solomon seems to say that time goes by swiftly and gets away from us; but God keeps track of it and will, at the end of time, call into account what we have done with time (12:14). This ties in with verses 16-17 where Solomon witnessed the injustices of his day and wondered why divine judgment was delayed.

"How can God be in control when there is so much evil in our world, with the wicked prospering in their sin and the righteous suffering in their obedience?" Solomon was not the first to raise that question, nor will he be the last. But once again, he comforted himself with two assurances: God has a time for everything, including judgment (see 8:6, 11); and God is working out His eternal purposes in and through the deeds of men, even the deeds of the wicked.

Yes, God will judge when history has run its course, *but God is judging now* (v. 18). In the experiences of life, God is testing man. (The word is "manifest" in the KJV. The Hebrew word means "to sift, to winnow.") God is revealing what man is really like; He is sifting man. For, when man leaves God out of his life, he becomes like an animal. (See Ps. 32:9; Prov. 7; 2 Peter 2:19-20.) He lives like a beast and dies like a beast.

We must be careful not to misinterpret verses 19-20 and draw the erroneous conclusion that there is no difference between men and animals. Solomon merely pointed out that men and beasts have two things in common: they both die and their bodies return to the dust (Gen. 2:7; 3:19). Being made in the image of God, man has a definite advantage over animals as far as life is concerned; but when it comes to the fact of death, man has no special advantage: he too turns to dust. Of course, people who are saved through faith in Christ will one day be resurrected to have glorified bodies suitable for the new heavenly home (1 Cor. 15:35ff).

The Bible says that death occurs when the spirit leaves the body (James 2:26, and see Gen. 35:18 and Luke 8:55). In verse 21, Solomon indicates that men and animals do not have the same experience at death, even though they both turn to dust after death. Man's spirit goes to God (see 12:7), while the spirit of a beast simply ceases to exist. You find a similar contrast expressed in Psalm 49.

The Preacher closed this section by reminding us again to accept life from God's hand and enjoy it while we can (v. 22). Nobody knows what the future holds; and even if we did know, we can't return to life after we have died and start to enjoy it again. (See 6:12, 7:14, 9:3.) Knowing that God is in sovereign control of life (3:1), we can submit to Him and be at peace.

> God holds the key of all unknown,
>   And I am glad;
> If other hands should hold the key,
> Or if He trusted it to me,
>   I might be sad.
>
> I cannot read His future plans,
>   But this I know:
> I have the smiling of His face,
> And all the refuge of His grace,
>   While here below.

(J. Parker)

Faith learns to live with seeming inconsistencies and absurdities, for we live by promises and not by explanations. We can't explain life, but we must experience life, either enduring it or enjoying it.

Solomon calls us to accept life, enjoy it a day at a time, and be satisfied. *We must never be satisfied with ourselves,* but we must be satisfied with what God gives to us in this life. If we grow in character and godliness, and if we live by faith, then we will be able to say with Paul, "I have learned to be content whatever the circumstances" (Phil. 4:11, NIV).

FIVE

Life Just Isn't Fair!

When Solomon first examined life "under the sun," his viewpoint was detached and philosophical (1:4-11); his conclusion was that life was meaningless and monotonous. But when he examined the question again, he went to where people really lived and discovered that life was not that simple. As he observed real people in real situations, the king had to deal with some painful facts, like life and death, time and eternity, and the final judgment.

Phillips Brooks, Anglican Bishop of Massachusetts a century ago, told ministerial students to read three "books": the Book of Books, the Bible; the book of nature; and the book of mankind. The ivory tower investigator will never have a balanced view of his subject if he remains in his ivory tower. Learning and living must be brought together.

In this chapter, Solomon recorded his observations from visiting four different places and watching several people go through a variety of experiences. His conclusion was that life is anything but monotonous, for we have no idea what problems may come to us on any given day. No wonder he wrote, "Do not boast about tomorrow, for you do not know what a day may bring forth" (Prov. 27:1, NKJV).

1. In the courtroom (Ecc. 4:1-3)

"Politics" has been defined as "the conduct of public affairs for private advantage." The nation of Israel had an adequate judicial system (Ex. 18:13-27; Deut. 17; 19), based on divine Law; but the system could be corrupted just like anything else (5:8). Moses warned officials to judge honestly and fairly (Lev. 19:15; Deut. 1:17), and both the prophet and the psalmist lashed out against social injustice (Ps. 82; Isa. 56:1; 59:1ff; Amos 1–2). Solomon had been a wise and just king (1 Kings 3:16-28), but it was impossible for him to guarantee the integrity of every officer in his government.

Solomon went into a courtroom to watch a trial, and there he saw innocent people being oppressed by power-hungry officials. The victims wept, but their tears did no good. Nobody stood with them to comfort or assist them. The oppressors had all the power and their victims were helpless to protest or ask for redress.

The American orator Daniel Webster once called justice "the ligament which holds civilized beings and . . . nations together." The "body politic" in Solomon's day had many a torn ligament!

The king witnessed three tragedies: (1) oppression and exploitation in the halls of justice; (2) pain and sorrow in the lives of innocent people; and (3) unconcern on the part of those who could have brought comfort. So devastated was Solomon by what he saw that he decided it was better to be dead than to be alive and oppressed. In fact, one was better off if never having been born at all. Then one would never have to see the evil works of sinful man.

Why didn't Solomon do something about this injustice? After all, he was the king. Alas, even the king couldn't do a great deal to solve the problem. For once Solomon started to interfere with his government and reorganize things, he would only create new problems and reveal more corruption. This is not to suggest that we today should despair of cleaning out political corruption. As Christian citizens, we must pray for all in authority (1 Tim. 2:1-6) and do what we can to see that just laws are passed and fairly enforced. But it's doubtful that a huge administrative body like the one in Israel would ever be free of corruption, or that a "crusader" could improve the situation.

Edward Gibbon, celebrated author of *The Decline and Fall of the Roman Empire,* said that political corruption was "the most infallible symptom of constitutional liberty." Perhaps he was right; for where there is freedom to obey, there is also freedom to disobey. Some of Solomon's officials decided they were above the law, and the innocent suffered.

2. In the marketplace (Ecc. 4:4-8)

Disgusted with what he saw in the "halls of justice," the king went down to the marketplace to watch the various laborers at work. Surely he would not be disappointed there, for honest toil is a gift from God. Even Adam had work to do in the Garden (Gen. 2:15), and our Lord was a carpenter when He was here on earth (Mark 6:3). Solomon considered four different kinds of men.

The industrious man (v. 4). It was natural for Solomon first to find a laborer who was working hard. For, after all, had not the king extolled the virtues of hard work in the Book of Proverbs? The man was not only busy, but he was skillful in his work and competent in all he did. He had mastered the techniques of his trade.

So much for the worker's *hands;* what about his *heart?* It was here that Solomon had his next disappointment. The only reason these people perfected their skills and worked hard at their jobs was to compete with others and make more money than their neighbors. The purpose of their work was not to produce beautiful or useful products, or to help people, but to stay ahead of the competition and survive in the battle for bread.

God did not put this "selfishness factor" into human labor; it's the result of sin in the human heart. We covet what others have; we not only want to have those things, but we want to go beyond and have even more. Covetousness, competition, and envy often go together. Competition is not sinful of itself, but when "being first" is more important than being honest, there will be trouble. Traditional rivalry between teams or schools can be a helpful thing, but when rivalry turns into riots, sin has entered the scene.

The idle man (vv. 5-6). Solomon moved from one extreme to the other and began to study a man who had no ambition at all. Perhaps the king could learn about life by examining the antithesis, the way scientists study cold to better understand heat. It must have been difficult for him to watch an idle man, because Solomon had no sympathy for lazy people who sat all day with folded hands and did nothing. (See Prov. 18:9, 19:15, 24:30-34.)

Solomon learned nothing he didn't already know: laziness is a slow comfortable path toward self-destruction. It may be pleasant to sleep late every morning and not have to go to work, but it's unpleasant not to have money to buy the necessities of life. "'Let me sleep a little longer!' Sure, just a little more! And as you sleep, poverty creeps upon you like a robber and destroys you; want attacks you in full armor" (Prov. 6:10-11, TLB). Paul stated it bluntly: "If any would not work, neither should he eat" (2 Thes. 3:10).

The industrious man was motivated by competition and caught in the rat race of life. He had no leisure time. The idle man was motivated by pleasure and was headed for ruin. He had no productive time. Is there no middle way between these two extremes? Yes, there is.

The integrated man (v. 6). Here was a man whose life was balanced: he was productive in his work, but he was also careful to take time for quietness. He did not run in the rat race, but neither did he try to run away from the normal responsibilities of life. A 1989 Harris survey revealed that the amount of leisure time enjoyed by the average American had shrunk 37 percent from 1973. This suggests that fewer people know how to keep life in balance. They are caught in the rat race and don't know how to escape.

Why have both hands full of profit if that profit costs you your peace of mind and possibly your health? Better to have gain in one hand and quietness in the other. When a heart is controlled by envy and rivalry, life becomes one battle after another (James 3:13–4:4, and see Prov. 15:16). Paul's instructions about money in 1 Timothy 6 is applicable here, especially verse 6, "But godliness with contentment is great gain."

The industrious man thinks that money will bring him peace, but he has no time to enjoy it. The idle man thinks that doing nothing will bring him peace, but his life-style only destroys him. The integrated man enjoys both his labor and the fruit of his labor and balances toil with rest. You can take what you want from life, *but you must pay for it.*

The independent man (vv. 7-8). Then Solomon noticed a solitary man, very hard at work, so he went to question him. The king discovered that the man had no relatives or partners to help him in his business, nor did he desire any help. He wanted all the profit for himself. But he was so busy, he had no time to enjoy his profits. And, if he died, he had no family to inherit his wealth. In other words, all his labor was in vain.

The Greek philosopher Socrates said, "The unexamined life is not worth living." But the independent man never stopped long enough to ask himself: "For whom am I working so hard? Why am I robbing myself of the enjoyments of life just to amass more and more money?" The industrious man was at least providing employment for people, and the idle man was enjoying some leisure, but the independent man was helping neither the economy nor himself.

Solomon's conclusion was, "This too is meaningless—a miserable business!" (v. 8, NIV) God wants us to labor, but to labor in the right spirit and for the right reasons. Blessed are the balanced!

3. On the highway (Ecc. 4:9-12)

Solomon's experience with the independent man caused him to consider the importance of friendship and the value of people doing things together. He may have recalled the Jewish proverb, "A friendless man is like a left hand bereft of the right." Perhaps he watched some pilgrims on the highway and drew the conclusion, "Two are better than one."

Two are certainly better than one when it comes to *working* (v. 9) because two workers can get more done. Even when they divide the profits, they still get a better return for their efforts than if they had worked alone. Also, it's much easier to do difficult jobs together because one can be an encouragement to the other.

Two are better when it comes to *walking* (v. 10). Roads and paths in Palestine were not paved or even leveled, and there were many hidden rocks in the fields. It was not uncommon for even the most experienced traveler to stumble and fall, perhaps break a bone, or even fall into a hidden pit (Ex. 21:33-34). How wonderful to have a friend who can help you up (or out). But if this applies to our *physical* falls, how much more does it apply to those times when we stumble in our *spiritual* walk and need restoration (Gal. 6:1-2)? How grateful we should be for Christian friends who help us walk straight.

Two are better than one when it comes to *warmth* (v. 11). Two travelers camping out, or even staying in the courtyard of a public inn, would feel the cold of the Palestinian night and need one another's warmth for comfort. The only way to be "warm alone" is to carry extra blankets and add to your load.

Finally, two are better than one when it comes to their

watchcare, especially at night (v. 12). "Though one may be overpowered, two can defend themselves" (v. 12, NIV). It was dangerous for anyone to travel alone, day or night; most people traveled in groups for fellowship and for safety. Even David was grateful for a friend who stepped in and saved the king's life (2 Sam. 21:15-17).

Solomon started with the number *one* (v. 8), then moved to *two* (v. 9), and then closed with *three* (v. 12). This is typical of Hebrew literature (Prov. 6:16; Amos 1:3, 6, 9, etc.). One cord could be broken easily; two cords would require more strength; but three cords woven together could not be easily broken. If two travelers are better than one, then three would fare even better. Solomon had more than numbers in mind; he was also thinking of the unity involved in three cords woven together—what a beautiful picture of friendship!

4. In the palace (Ecc. 4:13-16)

This is Solomon's fourth "better" statement (4:3, 6, 9), introducing a story that teaches two truths: the instability of political power and the fickleness of popularity. The king in the story had at one time heeded his counselors' advice and ruled wisely, but when he got old, he refused to listen to them. The problem was more than pride and senility. He was probably surrounded by a collection of "parasites" who flattered him, isolated him from reality, and took from him all they could get. This often happens to weak leaders who are more concerned about themselves than about their people.

There is a hero in the story, a wise youth who is in prison. Perhaps he was there because he tried to help the king and the king resented it. Or maybe somebody in the court lied about the youth. (That's what happened to Joseph. See Gen. 39.) At any rate, the youth got out of prison and became king. Everybody cheered the underdog and rejoiced that the nation at last had wise leadership.

Consider now what this story says. The young man was born poor, but he became rich. The old king was rich but it didn't make him any wiser, so he might just as well have been poor. The young man was in prison, but he got out and took the throne. The old king was imprisoned in his stupidity (and within his circle of sycophants) and lost his throne. So far, the moral of the story is: Wealth and position are no guarantee of success, and poverty and seeming failure are no barriers to achievement. The key is wisdom.

But the story goes on. Apparently the young man got out of prison and took the throne because of popular demand. "I have seen all the living under the sun throng to the side of the second lad who replaces him" [the old king] (v. 15, NASB). It looked like the new young king had it made, but alas, his popularity didn't last. "He can become the leader of millions of people, and be very popular. But, then, the younger generation grows up around him and rejects him!" (v. 16, TLB) The new crowd deposed the king and appointed somebody else.

Oliver Cromwell, who took the British throne away from Charles I and established the Commonwealth, said to a friend, "Do not trust to the cheering, for those persons would shout as much if you and I were going to be hanged." Cromwell understood crowd psychology!

Once again, Solomon drew the same conclusion: it is all "vanity and vexation of spirit" (see vv. 4 and 8).

No matter where Solomon went, no matter what aspect of life he studied, he learned an important lesson from the Lord. When he looked up, he saw that God was in control of life and balanced its varied experiences (3:1-8). When he looked within, he saw that man was made for eternity and that God would make all things beautiful in their time (3:9-14). When he looked ahead, he saw the last enemy, death. Then as he looked around (4:1-16), he understood that life is complex, difficult, and not easy to explain. One thing is sure: No matter where you look, you see trials and problems and people who could use some encouragement.

However, Solomon was not cynical about life. Nowhere does he tell us to get out of the race and retreat to some safe and comfortable corner of the world where nothing can bother us. Life does not stand still. Life comes at us full speed, without warning, and we must stand up and take it and, with God's help, make the most of it.

If this chapter teaches us anything, it is that we need one another because "two are better than one." Yes, there are some advantages to an independent life, but there are also disadvantages, and we discover them painfully as we get older.

The chapter also emphasizes balance in life. "Better is a handful with quietness than both hands full, together with toil and grasping for the wind" (v. 6, NKJV). It's good to have the things that money can buy, provided you don't lose the things that money can't buy. What is it really costing you *in terms of life* to get the things that are important to you? How much of the permanent are you sacrificing to get your hands on the temporary?

Or, to quote the words of Jesus: "For what shall it profit a man, if he shall gain the whole world, and lose his own soul? Or what shall a man give in exchange for his soul?" (Mark 8:36-37)

Stop, Thief!

The magazine cartoon showed a dismal looking man walking out of a bank manager's office with the manager saying to his secretary, "He suffers from back problems: back taxes, back rent, and back alimony."

Many people today suffer from similar "back problems." They refuse to heed the warning Bill Earle gave many years ago: "When your outgo exceeds your income, your upkeep will be your downfall."

The wealthy King Solomon knew something about money. Some of this wisdom he shared in the Book of Proverbs, and some he included here in Ecclesiastes. After all, he couldn't discuss "life under the sun" and ignore money!

But he goes beyond the subject of mere money and deals with the *values* of life, the things that really count. After all, there is more than one way to be rich and more than one way to be poor. In this chapter, Solomon issues three warnings that relate to the values of life.

1. Don't rob the Lord (Ecc. 5:1-7)

Solomon had visited the courtroom, the marketplace, the highway, and the palace. Now he paid a visit to the temple, that magnificent building whose construction he had supervised. He watched the worshipers come and go, praising God, praying, sacrificing, and making vows. He noted that many of them were not at all sincere in their worship, and they left the sacred precincts in worse spiritual condition than when they had entered. What was their sin? They were robbing God of the reverence and honor that He deserved. Their acts of worship were perfunctory, insincere, and hypocritical.

In today's language, "Keep thy foot!" means "Watch your step!" Even though God's glorious presence doesn't dwell in our church buildings as it did in the temple, believers today still need to heed this warning. *The worship of God is the highest ministry of the church and must come from devoted hearts and yielded wills.* For God's people to participate in public worship while harboring unconfessed sin is to ask for God's rebuke and judgment (Isa. 1:10-20; Amos 5; Ps. 50).

Solomon touched on several aspects of worship, the first of which was *the offering of sacrifices* (v. 1). God's people today don't offer animals to the Lord as in Old Testament times, because Jesus Christ has fulfilled all the sacrifices in His death on the cross (Heb. 10:1-14). But as the priests of God, believers today offer up spiritual sacrifices through Him: our bodies (Rom. 12:1-2); people won to the Saviour (Rom. 15:16); money (Phil. 4:18); praise and good works (Heb. 13:15-16); a broken heart (Ps. 51:17); and our prayers of faith (Ps. 141:1-2).

The important thing is that the worshiper "be more ready to hear," that is, to obey the Word of God. Sacrifices are not substitutes for obedience, as King Saul found out when he tried to cover up his disobedience with pious promises (1 Sam. 15:12-23). Offerings in the hands without obedient faith in the heart become "the sacrifice of fools," because *only a fool thinks he can deceive God.* The fool thinks he is doing good, but he or she is only doing evil. And God knows it.

Then Solomon issued a warning about *careless praying* (vv. 2-3). Prayer is serious business. Like marriage, "it must not be entered into lightly or carelessly, but soberly and in the fear of God." If you and I were privileged to bring our needs and requests to the White House or to Buckingham Palace, we would prepare our words carefully and exhibit proper behavior. How much more important it is when we come to the throne of Almighty God. Yet, there is so much flippant praying done by people who seem to know nothing about the fear of the Lord.

When you pray, watch out for both *hasty words* and *too many words* (Matt. 6:7). The secret of acceptable praying is a prepared heart (Ps. 141:1-2), because the mouth speaks what the heart contains (Matt. 12:34-37). If we pray only to impress people, we will not get through to God. The author of *Pilgrim's Progress,* John Bunyan, wrote: "In prayer, it is better to have a heart without words, than words without a heart."

Verse 3 presents an analogy: Just as many dreams show that the person sleeping is a hard worker, so many words show that the person praying is a fool (Prov. 29:20). I recall a church prayer meeting during which a young man prayed eloquently and at great length, but nobody sensed the power of God at work. When an uneducated immigrant stood up and stammered out her brief prayer in broken English, we all said a fervent "Amen!" We sensed that God had heard her requests. Spurgeon said, "It is not the length of our prayers, but the strength of our prayers, that makes the difference."

Solomon's third admonition had to do with *making vows to the Lord* (vv. 4-7). God did not require His people to make vows in order to be accepted by Him, but the opportunity was there for them to express their devotion if they felt led to do so (see Num. 30; Deut. 23:21-23; Acts 18:18).

The Preacher warned about two sins. The first was that of making the vow with no intention of keeping it, in other words, lying to God. The second sin was making the vow but delaying to keep it, hoping you could get out of it. When the priest ["angel" = messenger] came to collect the promised sacrifice or gift, the person would say, "Please forget about my vow! It was a mistake!"

God hears what we say and holds us to our promises, unless they were so foolish that He could only dismiss them. If providence prevents us from fulfilling what we promised, God understands and will release us. If we made our vows only to impress others, or perhaps to "bribe" the Lord ("If God answers my prayer, I will give $500 to missions!"), then we will pay for our careless words. Many times in my pastoral ministry I have heard sick people make promises to God as they asked for healing, only to see those promises forgotten when they recovered.

People make empty vows because they live in a religious "dream world"; they think that *words* are the same as *deeds* (v. 7). Their worship is not serious, so their words are not dependable. They enjoy the "good feelings" that come when they make their promises to God, but they do themselves more harm than good. They like to "dream" about fulfilling their vows, but they never get around to doing it. They practice a make-believe religion that neither glorifies God nor builds Christian character.

"I will go into thy house with burnt offerings; I will pay thee my vows, which my lips have uttered, and my mouth hath spoken, when I was in trouble" (Ps. 66:13-14). When we rob the Lord of the worship and honor due to Him, we are also robbing ourselves of the spiritual blessings He bestows on those who "worship Him in spirit and in truth" (John 4:24).

2. Don't rob others (Ecc. 5:8-9)

Solomon left the temple and went to the city hall where he again witnessed corrupt politicians oppressing the poor (3:16-

17; 4:1-3). The government officials violated the law by using their authority to help themselves and not to serve others, a practice condemned by Moses (Lev. 19:15; Deut. 24:17).

The remarkable thing is that Solomon wrote, "Don't be surprised at this!" He certainly did not approve of their unlawful practices, but he knew too much about the human heart to expect anything different from the complicated bureaucracy in Israel.

The NIV translation of verse 8 gives a vivid description of the situation: "One official is eyed by a higher one, and over them both are others higher still." Instead of the poor man getting a fair hearing, "the matter is lost in red tape and bureaucracy" (v. 8, TLB), and the various officials pocket the money that should have gone to the innocent poor man.

Verse 9 is difficult and major translations do not agree. The general idea seems to be that in spite of corruption in the bureaucracy, it is better to have organized government, and a king over the land, than to have anarchy. A few dishonest people may profit from corrupt practices, but *everybody* benefits from organized authority. Of course, the ideal is to have a government that is both honest and efficient, but man's heart being what it is, the temptation to dishonest gain is always there. Lord Acton wrote to Bishop Mandell Creighton in 1887, "Power tends to corrupt; absolute power corrupts absolutely." Solomon's investigation bears this out.

3. Don't rob yourself (Ecc. 5:10-20)
Solomon had already discussed "the futility of wealth" in 2:1-11, and some of those ideas are repeated here. What he did in this section was demolish several of the myths that people hold about wealth. Because they hold to these illusions, they rob themselves of the blessings God has for them.

Wealth brings satisfaction (v. 10). Some people treat money as though it were a god. They love it, make sacrifices for it, and think that it can do anything. Their minds are filled with thoughts about it; their lives are controlled by getting it and guarding it; and when they have it, they experience a great sense of security. What faith in the Lord does for the Christian, money does for many unbelievers. How often we hear people say, "Well, money may not be the number one thing in life, but it's way ahead of whatever is number two!"

The person who loves money cannot be satisfied no matter how much is in the bank account—because the human heart was made to be satisfied only by God (3:11). "Take heed and beware of covetousness," warned Jesus, "for one's life does not consist in the abundance of the things which he possesses" (Luke 12:15, NKJV). First the person loves money, and then he loves *more* money, and the disappointing pursuit has begun that can lead to all sorts of problems. "For the love of money is a root of all kinds of evil" (1 Tim. 6:10, NKJV).

Money solves every problem (v. 11). There is no escaping the fact that we need a certain amount of money in order to live in this world, but money *of itself* is not the magic "cure-all" for every problem. In fact, an increase in wealth usually creates new problems that we never even knew existed before. Solomon mentioned one: relatives and friends start showing up and enjoying our hospitality. All we can do is watch them eat up our wealth. Or perhaps it is the tax agent who visits us and decides that we owe the government more money.

John Wesley, cofounder of the Methodist Church, told his people, "Make all you can, save all you can, give all you can." Wesley himself could have been a very wealthy man, but he chose to live simply and give generously.

Wealth brings peace of mind (v. 12). The late Joe Louis, world heavyweight boxing champion, used to say, "I don't like money actually, but it quiets my nerves." But Solomon said that possessing wealth is no guarantee that your nerves will be calm and your sleep sound. According to him, the common laborer sleeps better than the rich man. The suggestion seems to be that the rich man ate too much and was kept awake all night by an upset stomach. But surely Solomon had something greater in mind than that. *The Living Bible* expresses verse 12 perfectly: "The man who works hard sleeps well whether he eats little or much, but the rich must worry and suffer insomnia."

More than one preacher has mentioned John D. Rockefeller in his sermons as an example of a man whose life was almost ruined by wealth. At the age of fifty-three, Rockefeller was the world's only billionaire, earning about a million dollars a week. But he was a sick man who lived on crackers and milk and could not sleep because of worry. When he started giving his money away, his health changed radically and he lived to celebrate his ninety-eighth birthday!

Yes, it's good to have the things that money can buy, provided you don't lose the things that money can't buy.

Wealth provides security (vv. 13-17). The picture here is of two rich men. One hoarded all his wealth and ruined himself by becoming a miser. The other man made some unsound investments and lost his wealth. He was right back where he started from and had no estate to leave to his son. He spent the rest of his days in the darkness of discouragement and defeat, and he did not enjoy life. Like all of us, he brought nothing into the world at birth, and he took nothing out of the world at death (see Job 1:21; Ps. 49:17; 1 Tim. 6:7).

This account makes us think of our Lord's parable about the Rich Fool (Luke 12:13-21). The man thought all his problems were solved when he became rich, but immediately he was faced with providing bigger barns for his wealth. He thought he was safe and secure for years to come, but that night he died! His money provided no security whatsoever.

Keep in mind that Solomon was advocating neither poverty nor riches, because both have their problems (Prov. 30:7-9).

The Preacher was warning his listeners against the love of money and the delusions that wealth can bring. In the closing verses of the chapter (vv. 18-20), he affirmed once again the importance of accepting our station in life and enjoying the blessings that God gives to us.

The thing that is "good and fitting" (v. 18, NKJV) is to labor faithfully, enjoy the good things of life, and accept it all as the gracious gift of God. Solomon gave us this wise counsel before in 2:24, 3:12-13, and 3:22, and he will repeat it at least three more times before he ends his "sermon."

There are three ways to get wealth: we can work for it, we can steal it, or we can receive it as a gift (see Eph. 4:28). Solomon saw the blessings of life as God's gift to those who work and who accept that work as the favor of God. "To enjoy your work and to accept your lot in life—that is indeed a gift from God" (v. 19, TLB).

Solomon added another important thought: the ability to *enjoy* life's blessings is also a gift from God. Solomon will expand on this thought in the next chapter and point out the unhappiness of people who possess wealth but are not able to enjoy it. We thank God for food, but we should also thank Him for healthy taste buds and a digestive system that functions correctly. A wealthy friend, now in heaven, often took me and my wife to expensive restaurants, but he was unable to enjoy the food because he couldn't taste it. All of his wealth could not purchase healing for his taste buds.

Verse 20 may mean that the person who rejoices in God's daily blessings will never have regrets. "The person who does that will not need to look back with sorrow on his past, for God gives him joy" (TLB). The time to start storing up happy memories is *now*. "So teach us to number our days, that we may apply our hearts unto wisdom" (Ps. 90:12).

It may also mean that the believer who gratefully accepts God's gifts today will not fret and worry about how long he or she will live. It is an established fact that the people who have the most birthdays live the longest, but if they keep complaining about "getting old" they will have very little to enjoy. People who are thankful to God "will not dwell overmuch upon the passing years," as the *New English Bible* translates verse 20. They will take each day as it comes and use it to serve the Lord.

In chapter 6, Solomon will conclude his discussion of "the futility of wealth." He might well have chosen Matthew 6:33 as the text for his message, "But seek first the kingdom of God and His righteousness, and all these things shall be added to you" (NKJV). The important thing is that we love the Lord, accept the lot He assigns us, and enjoy the blessings He graciously bestows.

If we focus more on the gifts than on the Giver, we are guilty of idolatry. If we accept His gifts, but complain about them, we are guilty of ingratitude. If we hoard His gifts and will not share them with others, we are guilty of indulgence. But if we yield to His will and use what He gives us for His glory, then we can enjoy life and be satisfied.

SEVEN

Is Life a Dead-End Street?

It's interesting to read the different expressions people use to picture *futility*. Solomon compared the futility of life to a soap bubble ("vanity of vanities") and to "chasing after the wind." I have read statements like: "As futile as watering a post." "As futile as plowing the rocks." "As futile as singing songs to a dead horse" (or "singing twice to a deaf man"). "As futile as pounding water with a mortar" (or "carrying water in a sieve").

In his poem *The Task,* the hymn writer William Cowper ("There Is A Fountain") pictured futility this way:

> The toil of dropping buckets into empty wells,
> and growing old in drawing nothing up.

If Cowper were alive today, he might look at our "automobile society" and write:

> As futile as blind men driving cars
> down crowded dead-end streets.

Is life a dead-end street? Sometimes it seems to be, especially when we don't reach our goals or when we reach our goals but don't feel fulfilled in our achievement. More than one person in the Bible became so discouraged with life that he either wanted to die or wished he had never been born. This includes Moses (Num. 11:15), Elijah (1 Kings 19:4), Job (3:21; 7:15), Jeremiah (8:3; 15:10), and Jonah (4:3). Even the great apostle Paul despaired of life during a particularly tough time in his life (2 Cor. 1:8-11).

Perhaps the basic problem is that life confronts us with too many mysteries we can't fathom and too many puzzles we can't solve. For life to be truly satisfying, it has to make sense. When it doesn't make sense, we get frustrated. If people can't see a purpose in life, especially when they go through deep suffering, they start to question God and even wonder if life is worthwhile.

In Ecclesiastes 6, Solomon discussed three of life's mysteries: riches without enjoyment (1-6), labor without satisfaction (7-9), and questions without answers (10-12).

1. Riches without enjoyment (Ecc. 6:1-6)
What a seeming tragedy it is to have all the resources for a satisfying life and yet not be able to enjoy them for one reason or another. More than one person has worked hard and looked forward to a comfortable retirement only to have a heart attack and become either an invalid or a statistic. Or perhaps the peace of retirement is shattered by a crisis in the family that begins to drain both money and strength. Why do these things happen?

Solomon mentioned this subject in 5:19 and hinted at it in 3:13. To him, it was a basic principle that nobody can truly enjoy the gifts of God apart from the God who gives the gifts. To enjoy the gifts without the Giver is idolatry, and this can never satisfy the human heart. Enjoyment without God is merely entertainment, and it doesn't satisfy. But enjoyment with God is enrichment and it brings true joy and satisfaction.

Verse 2 may describe a hypothetical situation, or it might have happened to somebody Solomon knew. The fact that God gave Solomon riches, wealth, and honor (2 Chron. 1:11) made the account even more meaningful to him. How fortunate a person would be to lack nothing, but how miserable if he or she could not enjoy the blessings of life.

What would prevent this person from enjoying life? Perhaps trouble in the home (Prov. 15:16-17; 17:1), or illness, or even death (Luke 12:20). The person described in verse 2 had no heir, so a stranger acquired the estate and enjoyed it. It all seems so futile.

What is Solomon saying to us? "Enjoy the blessings of God *now* and thank Him for all of them." Don't *plan* to live—start living now. Be satisfied with what He gives you and use it all for His glory.

Verses 3-6 surely deal with a hypothetical case, because nobody lives for two thousand years, and no monogamous marriage is likely to produce a hundred children. (Solomon's son Rehoboam had eighty-eight children, but he had eighteen wives and sixty concubines—like father, like son. See 2 Chronicles 11:21.) The Preacher was obviously exaggerating here in order to make his point: no matter how much you possess, if you don't possess the power to enjoy it, you might just as well never have been born.

Here is a man with abundant resources and a large family, both of which, to an Old Testament Jew, were marks of God's special favor. But his family does not love him, for when he died, he was not lamented. That's the meaning of "he has no burial" (see Jer. 22:18-19). His relatives stayed around him only to use his money (5:11), and they wondered when the old man would die. When he finally did die, his surviving relatives could hardly wait for the reading of the will.

The rich man was really poor. For some reason, perhaps

sickness, he couldn't enjoy his money. And he couldn't enjoy his large family because there was no love in the home. They didn't even weep when the man died. Solomon's conclusion was that it were better for this man had he never been born, or that he had been stillborn (see Job 3).

Among the Jews at that time, a stillborn child was not always given a name. That way, it would not be remembered. It was felt that this would encourage the parents to get over their sorrow much faster. "It [the child] comes without meaning, it departs in darkness, and in darkness its name is shrouded" (v. 4, NIV). In my pastoral ministry, broken-hearted parents and grandparents have sometimes asked, "Why did God even permit this child to be conceived if it wasn't going to live?" Solomon asked, "Why did God permit this man to have wealth and a big family if the man couldn't enjoy it?"

Some would argue that existence is better than nonexistence and a difficult life better than no life at all. Solomon might agree with them, for "a living dog is better than a dead lion" (9:4). But the problem Solomon faced was not whether existence is better than nonexistence, but whether there is any purpose behind the whole seemingly unbalanced scheme of things. As he examined life "under the sun," he could find no reason why a person should be given riches and yet be deprived of the power to enjoy them.

The ability to enjoy life comes from within. It is a matter of character and not circumstances. "I have learned, in whatsoever state I am, therewith to be content," Paul wrote to the Philippians (4:11). The Greek word *autarkes,* translated "content," carries the idea of "self-contained, adequate, needing nothing from the outside." Paul carried *within* all the resources needed for facing life courageously and triumphing over difficulties. "I can do all things through Christ who strengthens me" (Phil. 4:13, NKJV).

The 2,000-year-old man and the stillborn baby both ended

up in the same place—the grave. Once again, the Preacher confronted his listeners with the certainty of death and the futility of life without God. He was preparing them for "the conclusion of the matter" when he would wrap up the sermon and encourage them to trust God (11:9–12:14).

2. Labor without satisfaction (Ecc. 6:7-9)

Solomon had spoken about the rich man; now he discusses the situation of the poor man. Rich and poor alike labor to stay alive. We must either produce food or earn money to buy it. The rich man can let his money work for him, but the poor man has to use his muscles if he and his family are going to eat. But even after all this labor, the appetite of neither one is fully satisfied.

Why does a person eat? So that he can add years to his life. But what good is it for me to add years to my life *if I don't add life to my years?* I'm like the birds that I watch in the backyard. They spend all their waking hours either looking for food or escaping from enemies. (We have cats in our neighborhood.) These birds are not really *living;* they are only *existing.* Yet they are fulfilling the purposes for which the Creator made them—and they even sing about it!

Solomon is not suggesting that it's wrong either to work or to eat. Many people enjoy doing both. But if life consists *only* in working and eating, then we are being controlled by our appetites and that almost puts us on the same level as animals. As far as nature is concerned, self-preservation may be the first law of life, but we who are made in the image of God must live for something higher (John 12:20-28). In the new creation (2 Cor. 5:17), self-preservation may well be the first law of death (Mark 8:34-38).

Both questions in verse 8 are answered by "None!" If all you do is live to satisfy your appetite, then the wise man has no advantage over the fool, nor does the poor man have any advantage trying to better his situation and learning to get along with the rich. Solomon is not belittling either education or self-improvement. He is only saying that these things of themselves cannot make life richer. We must have something greater for which to live.

A century ago, when the United States was starting to experience prosperity and expansion, the American naturalist Henry David Thoreau warned that men were devising "improved means to unimproved ends." He should see our world today. We can send messages around the world in seconds, but do we have anything significant to say? We can transmit pictures even from the moon, but our TV screens are stained with violence, sex, cheap advertising, and even cheaper entertainment.

Verse 9 is Solomon's version of the familiar saying, "A bird in the hand is worth two in the bush." This proverb has been around for a long time. The Greek biographer Plutarch (46–120) wrote, "He is a fool who lets slip a bird in the hand for a bird in the bush." Solomon is saying, "It's better to have little and really enjoy it than to dream about much and never attain it." Dreams have a way of becoming nightmares if we don't come to grips with reality.

Is Solomon telling us that it's wrong to dream great dreams or have a burning ambition to accomplish something in life? Of course not, but we must take care that our ambition is motivated by the glory of God and not the praise of men. We must want to serve others and not promote ourselves. If we think our achievements will automatically bring satisfaction, we are wrong. True satisfaction comes when we do the will of God from the heart (Eph. 6:6). "My food," said Jesus, "is to do the will of Him who sent Me, and to accomplish His work" (John 4:34, NASB).

Yes, in the will of God there can be riches with enjoyment and labor with satisfaction. But we must accept His plan for our lives, receive His gifts gratefully, and enjoy each day as He enables us. "Thou wilt show me the path of life. In thy presence is fullness of joy; at thy right hand there are pleasures for evermore" (Ps. 16:11).

3. Questions without answers (Ecc. 6:10-12)

Thus far, Solomon has said that life is a dead-end street for two kinds of people: those who have riches but no enjoyment and those who labor but have no satisfaction. But he has tried to point out that true happiness is not the automatic result of making a good living; it is the blessed by-product of making a good life. If you devote your life only to the pursuit of happiness, you will be miserable; however, if you devote your life to doing God's will, you will find happiness as well.

The British essayist and poet Joseph Addison (1672–1718) wrote, "The grand essentials to happiness in this life are something to do, someone to love, and something to hope for." Addison probably didn't have Christianity in mind when he wrote that, but we have all three in Jesus Christ!

The Preacher was not finished. He knew that life was also a dead-end street for a third kind of person—the person who required answers to all of life's questions. Solomon was not condemning honest inquiry, because Ecclesiastes is the record of his own investigation into the meaning of life. Rather, Solomon was saying, "There are some questions about life that nobody can answer. But our ignorance must not be used as an excuse for skepticism or unbelief. Instead, our ignorance should encourage us to have faith in God. After all, we don't live on explanations; we live on promises."

It's been my experience in pastoral ministry that most explanations don't solve personal problems or make people feel better. When the physician explains an X-ray to a patient, his explanation doesn't bring healing, although it is certainly an essential step toward recovery. Suffering Job kept arguing with God and demanding an explanation for his plight. God never did answer his questions, because knowledge in the mind does not guarantee healing for the heart. That comes only when we put faith in the promises of God.

Without going into great detail, in verses 10-12 Solomon touches on five questions that people often ask.

Since "what's going to be is going to be," why bother to make decisions? Isn't it all predestined anyway? "Whatever exists has already been named, and what man is has been known" (v. 10a, NIV). To the Jewish mind, giving a name to something is the same as fixing its character and stating what the thing really is. During the time of creation, God named the things that He made; and nobody changed those designations. "Light" is "light" and not "darkness"; "day" is "day" and not "night." (See Isa. 5:20.)

Our name is "man"—Adam, "from the earth" (Gen. 2:7). Nobody can change that: we came from the earth and we will return to the earth (Gen. 3:19). "Man" by any other name would still be "man," made from the dust and eventually returning to the dust.

The fact that God has named everything does not mean that our world is a prison and we have no freedom to act. Certainly God can accomplish His divine purposes with or without our cooperation, but He invites us to work with Him. We cooperate with God as we accept the "names" He has given to things: sin is sin; obedience is obedience; truth is truth. If we alter these names, we move into a world of illusion and lose touch with reality. This is where many people are living today.

We are free to decide and choose our world, *but we are not free to change the consequences.* If we choose a world of illusion, we start living on substitutes, and there can be no satisfaction in a world of substitutes. "And this is eternal life, that they may know Thee, the only true God, and Jesus Christ whom Thou hast sent" (John 17:3, NASB). "And we know that the Son of God has come, and has given us understanding, in order that we might know Him who is true, and we are in Him who is true, in His Son Jesus Christ. This is the true God and eternal life" (1 John 5:20, NASB).

Why disagree with God? We can't oppose Him and win, can we? " . . . neither may he contend with him that is mightier than he" (v. 10b). The word translated "contend" also means "dispute." Solomon seems to say, "It just doesn't pay to argue with God or to fight God. This is the way life is, so just accept it and let God have His way. You can't win, and even if you do think you win, you ultimately lose."

But this is a negative view of the will of God. It gives the impression that God's will is a difficult and painful thing that should be avoided at all cost. Jesus said that God's will was the food that nourished and satisfied Him (John 4:32-34). It was meat, not medicine. The will of God comes from the heart of God and is an expression of the love of God. (See Ps. 33:11.) What God wills for us is best for us, because He knows far more about us than we do.

Why would anyone want to have his or her "own way" just for the privilege of exercising "freedom"? Insisting on having our own way isn't freedom at all; it's the worst kind of bondage. In fact, the most terrible judgment we could experience in this life would be to have God "give us up" and let us have our own way (Rom. 1:24, 26, 28).

God is free to act as He sees best. He is not a prisoner of His attributes, His creation, or His eternal purposes. You and I may not understand how God exercises His freedom, but it isn't necessary for us to know all. Our greatest freedom comes when we are lovingly lost in the will of God. Our Father in heaven doesn't feel threatened when we question Him, debate with Him, or even wrestle with Him, so long as we love His will and want to please Him.

What do we accomplish with all these words? Does talking

about it solve the problem? (v. 11). In fact, there are times when it seems like the more we discuss a subject, the less we really understand it. Words don't always bring light; sometimes they produce clouds and even darkness. "The more the words, the less the meaning"(v. 11, NIV). But this is where we need the Word of God and the wisdom He alone can give us. If some discussions appear useless and produce "vanity," there are other times when conversation leads us closer to the truth and to the Lord.

Who knows what is good for us? (v. 12). God does! And wise is the person who takes time to listen to what God has to say. Yes, life may seem to be fleeting and illusive, like a soap bubble ("vain") or a shadow, but "he who does the will of God abides forever" (1 John 2:17, NKJV).

Does anybody know what's coming next? (v. 12b). In spite of what the astrologers, prophets, and fortune tellers claim, nobody knows the future except God. It is futile to speculate. God gives us enough information to encourage us, but He does not cater to idle curiosity. One thing is sure: death is coming, and we had better make the best use of our present opportunities. That is one of the major themes in Ecclesiastes.

Solomon has discussed two of his arguments that life is not worth living: the monotony of life (3:1–5:9) and the futility of wealth (5:10–6:12). He has discovered that life "under the sun" can indeed be monotonous and empty, but it need not be *if we include God in our lives.* Life is God's gift to us, and we must accept what He gives us and enjoy it while we can (3:12-15, 22; 5:18-20).

Solomon will next take up his third argument, the vanity of man's wisdom (7:1–8:17), and discuss whether or not wisdom can make life any better. Though wisdom can't explain all the problems or answer all the questions, it is still a valuable ally on the journey of life.

How to Be Better Off

"Where ignorance is bliss, 'tis folly to be wise." Thomas Gray wrote those oft-quoted words in his poem "Ode on a Distant Prospect of Eton College." He pictured the students on the playing field and in the classroom, enjoying life because they were innocent of what lay ahead.

> Alas, regardless of their doom,
> The little victims play!
> No sense have they of ills to come,
> Nor care beyond today.

His conclusion was logical: at that stage in life, it is better to be ignorant and happy, because there will be plenty of time later to experience the sorrows that knowledge may bring.

> Yet ah! why should they know their fate?
> Since sorrow never comes too late,
> And happiness too swiftly flies.
> Thought would destroy their paradise.
> No more; where ignorance is bliss,
> 'Tis folly to be wise.

Solomon had come to a similar conclusion when he argued in 1:12-18 that wisdom did not make life worth living. "For in much wisdom is much grief," he wrote in 1:18, "and he that increaseth knowledge, increaseth sorrow."

But then the king took a second look at the problem and modified his views. In Ecclesiastes 7 and 8, he discussed the importance of wisdom in life ("wisdom" is found fourteen times in these two chapters); and he answered the question asked in 6:12, "For who knoweth what is good for man in this life?" The Preacher concluded that, though wisdom can't explain all of life's mysteries, it can make at least three positive contributions to our lives.

1. Wisdom can make life better (Ecc. 7:1-10)

"Better" is a key word in this chapter; Solomon used it at least eleven times. His listeners must have been shocked when they heard Solomon describe the "better things" that come to the life of the person who follows God's wisdom.

Sorrow is better than laughter (7:1-4). If given the choice, most people would rather go to a birthday party than to a funeral; but Solomon advised against it. Why? Because sorrow can do more good for the heart than laughter can. (The word "heart" is used four times in these verses.) Solomon was certainly not a morose man with a gloomy lifestyle. After all, it was King Solomon who wrote Proverbs 15:13, 15; 17:22—*and* the Song of Solomon! Laughter can be like medicine that heals the broken heart, but sorrow can be like nourishing food that strengthens the inner person. It takes both for a balanced life, but few people realize this. There is "a time to laugh" (Ecc. 3:4).

Let's begin with Solomon's bizarre statement that the day of one's death is better than the day of one's birth (v. 1). This generalization must not be divorced from his opening statement that a person's good reputation (name) is like a fragrant perfume. (There is a play on words here: "name" is *shem* in the Hebrew and "ointment" is *shemen.*) He used the same image in 10:1 and also in Song of Solomon 1:3.

Solomon was not contrasting *birth* and *death*, nor was he suggesting that it is better to die than to be born, because you can't die unless you have been born. He was contrasting two significant days in human experience: the day a person receives his or her name and the day when that name shows up in the obituary column. The life lived between those two events will determine whether that name leaves behind a lovely fragrance or a foul stench. "His name really stinks!" is an uncouth statement, but it gets the point across.

If a person dies with a good name, his or her reputation is sealed and the family need not worry. In that sense, the day of one's death is better than the day of one's birth. The life is over and the reputation is settled. (Solomon assumed that there were no hidden scandals.) "Every man has three names," says an ancient adage; "one his father and mother gave him, one others call him, and one he acquires himself."

"The memory of the just is blessed, but the name of the wicked shall rot" (Prov. 10:7, and see Prov. 22:1). Mary of Bethany anointed the Lord Jesus with expensive perfume and its fragrance filled the house. Jesus told her that her name would be honored throughout the world, and it is. On the other hand, Judas sold the Lord Jesus into the hands of the enemy; and his name is generally despised (Mark 14:1-11). When Judas was born, he was given the good name "Judah," which means "praise." It belonged to the royal tribe in Israel. By the time Judas died, he had turned that honorable name into something shameful.

In verses 2-4, Solomon advised the people to look death in the face and learn from it. He did not say that we should be *preoccupied* with death, because that could be abnormal. But there is a danger that we might try to avoid confrontations with the reality of death and, as a result, not take life as seriously as we should. "So teach us to number our days, that we may apply our hearts unto wisdom" (Ps. 90:12).

The Preacher is not presenting us with an either/or situation; he is asking for balance. The Hebrew word for "laughter" in verse 3 can mean "the laughter of derision or scorn." While there is a place for healthy humor in life, we must beware of the frivolous laughter that is often found in "the house of mirth" (v. 4). When people jest about death, for example, it is usually evidence that they are afraid of it and not prepared to meet it. They are running away.

The late Dr. Ernest Becker wrote in his Pulitzer Prize-winning book *The Denial of Death:* " . . . the idea of death, the fear of it, haunts the human animal like nothing else; it is a mainspring of human activity—activity designed largely to avoid the fatality of death, to overcome it by denying in some way that it is the final destiny for man" (Free Press, 1975, p. ix). King Solomon knew this truth centuries ago!

Rebuke is better than praise (7:5-6). King Solomon compared the praise of fools to the burning thorns in a campfire: you hear a lot of noise, but you don't get much lasting good. (Again, Solomon used a play on words. In the Hebrew, "song" is *shir,* "pot" is *sir,* and "thorns" is *sirim.*) If we allow it, a wise person's rebuke will accomplish far more in our lives than will the flattery of fools. Solomon may have learned this truth from his father (Ps. 141:5), and he certainly emphasized it when he wrote the Book of Proverbs (10:17; 12:1; 15:5; 17:10; 25:12; 27:5, 17; 29:1, 15).

The British literary giant Samuel Johnson was at the home of the famous actor David Garrick, and a "celebrated lady" persisted in showering Johnson with compliments. "Spare me, I beseech you, dear madam!" he replied; but, as his biographer Boswell put it, "She still laid it on." Finally Johnson silenced her by saying, "Dearest lady, consider with yourself what your flattery is worth, before you bestow it so freely."

The "long haul" is better than the shortcut (7:7-9). Beware of "easy" routes; they often become expensive detours that are difficult and painful. In 1976, my wife and I were driving through Scotland, and a friend mapped out a "faster" route from Balmoral Castle to Inverness. It turned out to be a hazardous one-lane road that the local people called "The Devil's Elbow," and en route we met a bus and a cement truck! "Watch and pray" was our verse for that day.

Bribery appears to be a quick way to get things done (v. 7), but it only turns a wise man into a fool and encourages the corruption already in the human heart. Far better that we wait patiently and humbly for God to work out His will than that we get angry and demand our own way (v. 8). See also Proverbs 14:17, 16:32, and James 1:19.

"Better is the end of a thing than the beginning" applies when we are living according to God's wisdom. The beginning of sin leads to a terrible end—death (James 1:13-15), but if God is at the beginning of what we do, He will see to it that we reach the ending successfully (Phil. 1:6; Heb. 12:2). The Christian believer can claim Romans 8:28 because he knows that God is at work in the world, accomplishing His purposes.

An Arab proverb says, "Watch your beginnings." Good beginnings will usually mean good endings. The Prodigal Son started with happiness and wealth, but ended with suffering and poverty (Luke 15:11-24). Joseph began as a slave but ended up a sovereign! God always saves "the best wine" until the last (John 2:10), but Satan starts with his "best" and then leads the sinner into suffering and perhaps even death.

Today is better than yesterday (7:10). When life is difficult and we are impatient for change, it is easy to long for "the good old days" when things were better. When the foundation was laid for the second temple, the old men wept for "the good old days" and the young men sang because the work had begun

(Ezra 3:12-13). It has been said that "the good old days" are the combination of a bad memory and a good imagination, and often this is true.

Yesterday is past and cannot be changed, and tomorrow may not come; so make the most of today. *"Carpe diem!"* wrote the Roman poet Horace. "Seize the day!" This does not mean we shouldn't learn from the past or prepare for the future, because both are important. It means that we must live *today* in the will of God and not be paralyzed by yesterday or hypnotized by tomorrow. The Victorian essayist Hilaire Belloc wrote, "While you are dreaming of the future or regretting the past, the present, which is all you have, slips from you and is gone."

2. Wisdom helps us see life clearly (Ecc. 7:11-18)

One of the marks of maturity is the ability to look at life in perspective and not get out of balance. When you have God's wisdom, you will be able to accept and deal with the changing experiences of life.

Wealth (7:11-12). Wisdom is better than a generous inheritance. Money can lose its value, or be stolen; but true wisdom keeps its value and cannot be lost, unless we become fools and abandon it deliberately. The person who has wealth but lacks wisdom will only waste his fortune, but the person who has wisdom will know how to get and use wealth. We should be grateful for the rich treasure of wisdom we have inherited from the past, and we should be ashamed of ourselves that we too often ignore it or disobey it. Wisdom is like a "shelter" to those who obey it; it gives greater protection than money.

Providence (7:13). The rustic preacher who said to his people, "Learn to cooperate with the inevitable!" knew the meaning of this verse. *The Living Bible* paraphrases it, "See the way God does things and fall into line. Don't fight the facts of nature." This is not a summons to slavish fatalism; like Ecclesiastes 1:15, it is a sensible invitation to a life yielded to the will of God. If God makes something crooked, He is able to make it straight; and perhaps He will ask us to work with Him to get the job done. But if He wants it to stay crooked, we had better not argue with Him. We don't fully understand all the works of God (11:5), but we do know that "He hath made everything beautiful in its time" (3:11). This includes the things we may think are twisted and ugly.

While I don't agree with all of his theology, I do appreciate the "Serenity Prayer" written in 1934 by Reinhold Niebuhr. A version of it is used around the world by people in various support groups, such as Alcoholics Anonymous; and it fits the lesson Solomon teaches in verse 13:

> O God, give us
> Serenity to accept what cannot be changed,
> Courage to change what should be changed,
> And wisdom to distinguish the one from the
> other.

Adversity and prosperity (7:14). Wisdom gives us perspective so that we aren't discouraged when times are difficult or arrogant when things are going well. It takes a good deal of spirituality to be able to accept prosperity as well as adversity, for often prosperity does greater damage (Phil. 4:10-13). Job reminded his wife of this truth when she told him to curse God and die: "What? Shall we receive good at the hand of God, and shall we not receive evil [trouble]?" (2:10) Earlier, Job had said, "The Lord gave, and the Lord hath taken away; blessed be the name of the Lord" (1:21).

God balances our lives by giving us enough blessings to keep us happy and enough burdens to keep us humble. If all we had were blessings in our hands, we would fall right over, so the Lord balances the blessings in our hands with burdens on our backs. That helps to keep us steady, and as we yield to Him, He can even turn the burdens into blessings.

Why does God constitute our lives in this way? The answer is simple: to keep us from thinking we know it all and that we can manage our lives by ourselves. "Therefore, a man cannot discover anything about his future" (v. 14, NIV). Just about the time we think we have an explanation for things, God changes the situation and we have to throw out our formula. This is where Job's friends went wrong: they tried to use an old road map to guide Job on a brand new journey, and the map didn't fit. No matter how much experience we have in the Christian life, or how many books we read, we must still walk by faith.

Righteousness and sin (7:15-18). If there is one problem in life that demands a mature perspective, it is "Why do the righteous suffer and the wicked prosper?" The good die young while the wicked seem to enjoy long lives, and this seems contrary to the justice of God and the Word of God. Didn't God tell the people that the obedient would live long (Ex. 20:12; Deut. 4:40) and the disobedient would perish? (Deut. 4:25-26; Ps. 55:23)

Two facts must be noted. Yes, God did promise to bless Israel in their land if they obeyed His law, but He has not given those same promises to believers today under the new covenant. Francis Bacon (1561–1626) wrote, "Prosperity is the blessing of the Old Testament; adversity is the blessing of the New." Our Lord's opening words in the Sermon on the Mount were not "Blessed are the rich in substance" but "Blessed are the poor in spirit" (Matt. 5:3, and see Luke 6:20).

Second, the wicked appear to prosper *only if you take the short view of things.* This was the lesson Asaph recorded in Psalm 73 and that Paul reinforced in Romans 8:18 and 2 Corinthians 4:16-18. "They have their reward" (Matt. 6:2, 5, 16), and that reward is all they will ever get. They may gain the whole world, but they lose their own souls. This is the fate of all who follow their example and sacrifice the eternal for the temporal.

Verses 16-18 have been misunderstood by those who say that Solomon was teaching "moderation" in everyday life: don't be too righteous, but don't be too great a sinner. "Play it safe!" say these cautious philosophers, but this is not what Solomon wrote.

In the Hebrew text, the verbs in verse 16 carry the idea of reflexive action. Solomon said to the people, "Don't claim to be righteous and don't claim to be wise." In other words, he was warning them against *self-righteousness and the pride that comes when we think we have "arrived" and know it all.* Solomon made it clear in verse 20 that there are no righteous people, so he cannot be referring to true righteousness. He was condemning the self-righteousness of the hypocrite and the false wisdom of the proud, and he warned that these sins led to destruction and death.

Verse 18 balances the warning: we should take hold of true righteousness and should not withdraw from true wisdom, and the way to do it is to walk in the fear of God. "The fear of the Lord is the beginning of wisdom" (Prov. 9:10) and Jesus Christ is to the believer "wisdom and righteousness" (1 Cor. 1:30), so God's people need not "manufacture" these blessings themselves.

3. Wisdom helps us face life stronger (Ecc. 7:19-29)
"Wisdom makes one wise man more powerful than ten rulers in a city" (v. 19, NIV). The wise person fears the Lord and therefore does not fear anyone or anything else (Ps. 112). He walks with the Lord and has the adequacy necessary to face the challenges of life, including war (see 9:13-18).

What are some of the problems in life that we must face and overcome? Number one on the list is *sin,* because nobody on earth is sinless (v. 20, and note 1 Kings 8:46). We are all guilty of both sins of omission ("doeth good") and sins of commission ("sinneth not"). If we walk in the fear of God and follow His wisdom, we will be able to detect and defeat the wicked one when he comes to tempt us. Wisdom will guide us and guard us in our daily walk.

Another problem we face is *what people say about us* (vv. 21-22). The wise person pays no attention to the gossip of the day because he has more important matters which to attend. Charles Spurgeon told his pastoral students that the minister ought to have one blind eye and one deaf ear. "You cannot stop people's tongues," he said, "and therefore the best thing to do is to stop your own ears and never mind what is spoken. There is a world of idle chitchat abroad, and he who takes note of it will have enough to do" (*Lectures To My Students;* Marshall, Morgan, and Scott reprint edition, 1965; p. 321). Of course, if we are honest, we may have to confess that we have done our share of talking about others! See Psalm 38 and Matthew 7:1-3.

A third problem is *our inability to grasp the meaning of all that God is doing in this world* (vv. 23-25, and see 3:11 and 8:17). Even Solomon with all his God-given wisdom could not understand all that exists, how God manages it, and what purposes He has in mind. He searched for the "reason [scheme] of things" but found no final answers to all his questions. However, the wise man knows that he does not know, and this is what helps to make him wise!

Finally, the wise person must deal with *the sinfulness of humanity in general* (vv. 26-29). Solomon began with the sinful woman, the prostitute who traps men and leads them to death (v. 26, and see Prov. 2:16-19; 5:3-6; 6:24-26; and 7:5-27). Solomon himself had been snared by many foreign women who enticed him away from the Lord and into the worship of heathen gods (1 Kings 11:3-8). The way to escape this evil woman is to fear God and seek to please Him.

Solomon concluded that the whole human race was bound by sin and one man in a thousand was wise—and not one woman! (The number 1,000 is significant in the light of 1 Kings 11:3.) We must not think that Solomon rated women as less intelligent than men, because this is not the case. He spoke highly of women in Proverbs (12:4; 14:1; 18:22; 19:14; and 31:10ff), Ecclesiastes (9:9), and certainly in the Song of Solomon. In the Book of Proverbs, Solomon even pictured God's wisdom as a beautiful woman (1:20ff; 8:1ff; 9:1ff). But keep in mind that women in that day had neither the freedom nor the status that they have today, and it would be unusual for a woman to have learning equal to that of a man. It was considered a judgment of God for women to rule over the land (Isa. 3:12, but remember Miriam and Deborah, two women who had great leadership ability).

God made man (Adam) upright, but Adam disobeyed God and fell and now all men are sinners who seek out many clever inventions. Created in the image of God, man has the ability to understand and harness the forces God put into nature, but he doesn't always use this ability in constructive ways. Each forward step in science seems to open up a Pandora's box of new problems for the world, until we now find ourselves with the problems of polluted air and water and depleated natural resources. And beside that, man has used his abilities to devise alluring forms of sin that are destroying individuals and nations.

Yes, there are many snares and temptations in this evil world, but the person with godly wisdom will have the power to overcome. Solomon has proved his point: wisdom can make our lives better and clearer and stronger. We may not fully understand all that God is doing, but we will have enough wisdom to live for the good of others and the glory of God.

What About the Wicked?

As King Solomon continued to investigate the value of wisdom, he came face to face with the problem of evil in the world, a problem that no thinking person can honestly avoid. It is not *unbelief* that creates this problem, but *faith*. If there is no God, then we have nobody to blame but ourselves (or fate) for what happens in the world. But if we believe in a good and loving God, we must face the difficult question of why there is so much suffering in the world. Does God know about it and yet not care? Or does He know and care but lack the power to do anything about it?

Some people ponder this question and end up becoming either agnostics or atheists, but in so doing, they create a whole new problem: "Where does all the *good* come from in the world?" It's difficult to believe that matter *alone* produced the beautiful and enjoyable things we have in our world, even in the midst of so much evil.

Other people solve the problem by saying that evil is only an illusion and we shouldn't worry about it, or that God is in the process of "evolving" and can't do much about the tragedies of life. They assure us that God will get stronger and things will improve as the process of evolution goes on.

Solomon didn't deny the existence of God or the reality of evil, nor did he limit the power of God. Solomon solved the problem of evil by affirming these factors *and seeing them in their proper perspective.* We must not forget that one major source of evil in this world is fallen man and his "many devices," both good and evil, that have helped to create problems of one kind or another (7:29, NASB). God certainly can't be blamed for that!

During the darkest days of World War II, somebody asked a friend of mine, "Why doesn't God stop the war?" My friend wisely replied, "Because He didn't start it in the first place." Solomon would have agreed with that answer.

The Preacher explored the problem of evil in the world by examining three key areas of life.

1. Authority (Ecc. 8:1-9)

Beginning with Nimrod (Gen. 10:8-9) and continuing over the centuries through Pharaoh, Sennacherib, Nebuchadnezzar, Darius, the Caesars, and the latest petty dictator, millions of good people have been oppressed in one way or another by bad rulers. The Jews often suffered at the hands of foreign oppressors, and Solomon himself had been guilty of putting his own people under a heavy yoke of bondage (1 Kings 4:7-28; 12:1ff).

Keep in mind that Eastern rulers in that day held the power of life and death in their hands and often used that power capriciously. They were not elected by the people nor were they answerable to them. Some leaders ruled as benevolent dictators, but for the most part rulers in the ancient East were tyrannical despots who permitted nothing to stand in the way of fulfilling their desires.

Solomon described an officer in the royal court, a man who had to carry out the orders of a despotic ruler. The officer had wisdom; in fact, it showed on his face (v. 1, and see Neh. 2:1ff and Prov. 15:13). Suppose the king commanded the servant to do something evil, something that the servant did not want to do? What should the servant do? Here is where wisdom comes to his aid. His wisdom told him that there were four possible approaches he could take to this problem.

Disobedience. But Solomon's admonition was, "Keep the king's commandment" (v. 2). Why? To begin with, the officer must be true to his oath of allegiance to the king and to God, who is the source of all authority in this world (Rom. 13). To disobey orders would mean breaking his promise to the ruler and to God, and that has serious consequences.

The king's word would have more power than the word of his servant (v. 4) and was bound to prevail, even if the king had to eliminate the opposition. Nobody could safely question the ruler's decisions because "the king can do no wrong." There was no law that could find the king guilty.

Third, the officer should obey orders so that he might avoid punishment (v. 5a). After all, his disobedience could lead to his death (see Dan. 4). Paul used a similar argument in Romans 13:3-4. We all have enough misery, so why add to it (v. 7)? Furthermore, since nobody can predict the future, we don't know how the king will respond to our decisions.

One thing is sure: a day is coming when wickedness will be judged (v. 8b), and even kings will not escape. Nobody can control the wind or prevent the day of his death ("wind" and "spirit" are the same word in the Hebrew), and nobody can get discharged from the army when a war is on. Likewise, nobody can stop the inexorable working of God's law, "Whatever a man sows, that he will also reap" (Gal. 6:7, NKJV). "Be sure your sin will find you out" (Num. 32:23).

But suppose the servant simply cannot obey his master? Then the servant must consider the other possibilities.

Desertion (v. 3a). You can just see the officer leaving the king's presence in disgust and giving up his position in court.

Even this action may not be safe since the king might be offended and punish the man anyway. But more than one person has quit a job or resigned from office in order to maintain his or her integrity. I recall chatting with a Christian press operator who left a fine job with a large printing firm because the company had decided to start printing pornographic magazines. He lost some income, but he kept his character.

Defiance (v. 3b). "Do not stand up for a bad cause" (NIV) can mean "Don't promote the king's evil plan" or "Don't get involved in a plan to overthrow the king." I prefer the second interpretation because it goes right along with the first admonition in verse 3. The officer rushes from the king's presence, finds others who are opposed to the king's plans, and with them begins to plot against the crown. Solomon did not approve of this approach.

Is there ever a place for "civil disobedience" in the life of the believer? Do law-abiding citizens have the right to resist authority when they feel the law is not just? Thomas Jefferson wrote, "Resistance to tyrants is obedience to God." Was he right?

When it comes to matters of conscience and the law, devoted believers have pretty much agreed with Peter: "We ought to obey God rather than men" (Acts 5:29). Christian prisoners and martyrs down through the ages testify to the courage of conscience and the importance of standing up for what is right. This doesn't mean we can resist the law on every minor matter that disturbs us, but it does mean we have the obligation to obey our conscience. How we express our disagreement with the authorities demands wisdom and grace; this is where the fourth possibility comes in.

Discernment (vv. 5b-6). The wise servant understands that "time and judgment [procedure, NASB]" must be considered in everything we do, because it takes discernment to know the right procedure for the right time. The impulsive person who overreacts and storms out of the room (v. 3) is probably only making the problem worse. Wisdom helps us understand people and situations and to figure out the right thing to do at the right time. "The wise heart will know the proper time and procedure" (v. 5b, NIV).

This is illustrated beautifully in the lives of several Old Testament believers. Joseph didn't impulsively reveal to his brothers who he was, because he wanted to be sure their hearts were right with their father and their God. Once he heard them confess their sins, Joseph knew it was the right time to identify himself. His handling of this delicate matter was a masterpiece of wisdom (see Gen. 43–45).

Nehemiah was burdened to rebuild the walls of Jerusalem, but he was not sure the king would release him for the task (Neh. 1–2). He waited and watched and prayed, knowing that God would one day open the way for him. When the opportune hour came, Nehemiah was ready and the king granted him his request. Nehemiah knew how to discern "time and procedure."

A prisoner of war in a Gentile land, Daniel refused to eat the unclean food set before him, but he didn't make a big scene about it. Instead, he exercised gentleness and wisdom by suggesting that the guards permit the Jews to experiment with a different diet. The plan worked and Daniel and his friends not only kept themselves ceremonially clean, but they were promoted in the king's court (see Dan. 1).

The apostles exercised spiritual discernment when they were arrested and persecuted (Acts 4–5). They showed respect toward those in authority even though the religious leaders were prejudiced and acted illegally. The apostles were even willing to suffer for their faith and the Lord honored them.

We have the options of disobeying, running away, defying orders, and even fighting back. But before we act, we must first exercise wisdom and seek to discern the right "time and procedure." It's not easy to be a consistent Christian in this complicated evil world, but we can ask for the wisdom of God and receive it by faith (James 1:5; 3:17-18).

2. Inequity (Ecc. 8:10-14)

Solomon summarized his concern in verse 14: "righteous men who get what the wicked deserve, and wicked men who get what the righteous deserve" (NIV). In spite of good laws and fine people who seek to enforce them, there is more injustice in this world than we care to admit. A Spanish proverb says, "Laws, like the spider's web, catch the fly and let the hawks go free." According to famous trial lawyer F. Lee Bailey, "In America, an acquittal doesn't mean you're innocent; it means you beat the rap." His definition is a bit cynical, but poet Robert Frost defined a jury as "twelve persons chosen to decide who has the better lawyer."

In verse 10, Solomon reported on a funeral he had attended. The deceased was a man who had frequented the temple ("the place of the holy") and had received much praise from the people, but he had not lived a godly life. Yet he was given a magnificent funeral, with an eloquent eulogy, while the truly godly people of the city were ignored and forgotten.

As he reflected on the matter, Solomon realized that the deceased man had continued in his sin because he thought he was getting away with it (v. 11). God is indeed longsuffering toward sinners and doesn't always judge sin immediately (2 Peter 3:1-12). However, God's mercy must not be used as an excuse for man's rebellion.

The Preacher concluded that the wicked will eventually be judged and the righteous will be rewarded (vv. 12-13), so it is better to fear the Lord and live a godly life. The evil man may live longer than the godly man. He may appear to get away with sin after sin, but the day of judgment will come and the wicked man will not escape. It is wisdom that points the way; for "the fear of the Lord is the beginning of wisdom" (Prov. 9:10).

No matter how long or full the wicked man's life may seem to be, it is only prolonged like a shadow and has no substance (v. 13). In fact, the shadows get longer as the sun is setting. Solomon may be suggesting that the long life of the wicked man is but a prelude to eternal darkness. What good is a long life if it is only a shadow going into the blackness of darkness forever (Jude 13)?

How should the wise person respond to the inequities and injustices in this world? Certainly we should do all we can to encourage the passing of good laws and the enforcement of them by capable people, but even this will not completely solve the problem. Until Jesus Christ sets up His righteous kingdom, there will always be injustices in our world. It is one of the "vanities" of life, and we must accept it without becoming pessimistic or cynical.

3. Mystery (Ecc. 8:15-17)

The person who has to know everything, or who thinks he knows everything, is destined for disappointment in this world. Through many difficult days and sleepless nights, the Preacher applied himself diligently to the mysteries of life. He came to the conclusion that "man cannot find out the work that is done under the sun" (v. 17; see 3:11; 7:14, 24, 27-28). Perhaps we can solve a puzzle here and there, but no man or woman can comprehend the totality of things or explain all that God is doing.

Historian Will Durant surveyed human history in his multivolume *Story of Civilization* and came to the conclusion that "our knowledge is a receding mirage in an expanding desert of ignorance." Of course, this fact must not be used as an excuse for stupidity. "The secret things belong unto the Lord our

God; but those things which are revealed belong unto us and to our children forever, that we may do all the words of this law" (Deut. 29:29). God doesn't expect us to know the unknowable, but He does expect us to learn all that we can and obey what He teaches us. In fact, the more we obey, the more He will teach us (John 7:17).

A confession of ignorance is the first step toward true knowledge. "And if anyone thinks that he knows anything, he knows nothing yet as he ought to know" (1 Cor. 8:2, NKJV). The person who wants to learn God's truth must possess honesty and humility. Harvard philosopher Alfred North Whitehead said, "Not ignorance, but ignorance of ignorance, is the death of knowledge."

The French philosopher Blaise Pascal wrote in his famous *Pensees* (#446): "If there were no obscurity, man would not feel his corruption; if there were no light, man could not hope for a cure. Thus it is not only right but useful for us that God should be partly concealed and partly revealed, since it is equally dangerous for man to know God without knowing his own wretchedness as to know his wretchedness without knowing God."

For the fourth time, Solomon told his congregation to enjoy life and delight in the fruit of their labors (v. 15; see 2:24; 3:12-15; and 5:18-20). Remember, this admonition is not the foolish "eat, drink, and be merry" philosophy of the unbelieving hedonist. Rather, it is the positive "faith outlook" of God's children who accept life as God's special gift and know that He gives us "all things richly to enjoy" (1 Tim. 6:17). Instead of complaining about what we don't have, we give thanks for what we do have and enjoy it.

This ends Solomon's re-examination of "the vanity of wisdom" (1:12-18). Instead of rejecting wisdom, the king concluded that wisdom is important to the person who wants to get the most out of life. While wisdom can't explain every mystery or solve every problem, it can help us exercise discernment in our decisions. "Yes, there is a time and a way for everything" (8:6, TLB), and the wise person knows what to do at just the right time.

T E N

ECCLESIASTES 9

Meeting Your Last Enemy

"Oh why do people waste their breath
Inventing dainty names for death?"

John Betjeman, the late Poet Laureate of England, wrote those words in his poem "Graveyards." Every honest person can answer the question, as Betjeman did in his poem: we invent "dainty names" because we don't want to face up to the reality of death. Sociologist Ernest Becker claimed "that of all things that move men, one of the principal ones is his terror of death" (*The Denial of Death*, p. 11).

During many years of pastoral ministry, I have seen this denial in action. When visiting bereaved families, I have noticed how often people deliberately avoid the word "death" and substitute phrases like "left us," "went home," "went to sleep," or "passed on." Of course, when a Christian dies, he or she does "go to sleep" and "go home," but this assurance should not make death any less real in our thinking or our feeling. The person who treats death lightly may fear death the most. If we take life seriously—and we should—then we can't treat death flippantly.

This is not the first time the subject of death has come into

Solomon's discourse, nor will it be the last. (See 1:4; 2:14-17; 3:18-20; 4:8; 5:15-16; 6:6; 8:8; 12:1-7.) After all, the only way to be prepared to live is to be prepared to die. Death is a fact of life, and Solomon examined many facets of life so that he might understand God's pattern for satisfied living. Robert E. Lee's last words were, "Let the tent be struck!" Unless Jesus Christ returns and takes us to heaven, we will one day "strike our tent" (2 Cor. 5:1-8) and leave the battlefield for a better land. We must be ready.

In this chapter, Solomon drew two conclusions: death is unavoidable (1-10) and life is unpredictable (11-18). That being the case, the best thing we can do is trust God, live by faith, and enjoy whatever blessings God gives us.

1. Death is unavoidable (Ecc. 9:1-10)

"I'm not afraid to die;" quipped Woody Allen, "I just don't want to be there when it happens." But he *will* be there when it happens, as must every human being, because there is no escaping death when your time has come. Death is not an accident, it's an appointment (Heb. 9:27), a destiny that nobody but God can cancel or change.

Life and death are "in the hand of God" (v. 1), and only He knows our future, whether it will bring blessing ("love") or sorrow ("hatred"). Solomon was not suggesting that we are passive actors in a cosmic drama, following an unchangeable script handed to us by an uncaring director. Throughout this book, Solomon has emphasized our freedom of discernment and decision. But only God knows what the future hold for us and what will happen tomorrow because of the decisions we make today.

"As it is with the good man, so with the sinner." (v. 2, NIV). If so, why bother to live a godly life?" someone may ask. "After all, whether we obey the Law or disobey, bring sacrifices or neglect them, make or break promises, we will die just the same." Yes, we share a common destiny on earth—death and the grave—*but we do not share a common destiny in eternity*. For that reason, everybody must honestly face "the last enemy" (1 Cor. 15:26) and decide how to deal with it. Christians have trusted Jesus Christ to save them from sin and death; so, as far as they are concerned, "the last enemy" has been defeated (Rom. 6:23; John 11:25-26; 1 Thess. 4:13-18; 1 Cor. 15:51-58). Unbelievers don't have that confidence and are unprepared to die.

How people deal with the reality of death reveals itself in the way they deal with the realities of life. Solomon pointed out three possible responses that people make to the ever-present fear of death.

Escape (v. 3). The fact of death and the fear of death will either bring out the best in people or the worst in people; and too often it is the worst. When death comes to a family, it doesn't *create* problems; it *reveals* them. Many ministers and funeral directors have witnessed the "X-ray" power of death and bereavement as it reveals the hearts of people. In facing the death of others, we are confronted with our own death, and many people just can't handle it.

"The heart of the sons of men is full of evil," and that evil is bound to come out. People will do almost *anything but repent* in order to escape the reality of death. They will get drunk, fight with their relatives, drive recklessly, spend large amounts of money on useless things, and plunge into one senseless pleasure after another, all to keep the Grim Reaper at arm's length. But their costly endeavors only distract them from the battle; they don't end the war, because "the last enemy" is still there.

Those of us who were privileged to have the late Joseph Bayly as our friend know what a positive attitude he had toward death. He and his wife had been through the valley many times and God used them to bring comfort and hope to other sorrowing pilgrims. His book *The Last Thing We Talk About* (David C. Cook Pub. Co.) is a beautiful testimony of how Jesus Christ can heal the brokenhearted. "Death is the great adventure," said Joe, "beside which moon landings and space trips pale into insignificance."

You don't get that kind of confidence by trying to run away from the reality of death. You get it by facing "the last enemy" honestly, turning from sin and trusting Jesus Christ to save you. Have you done that?

Endurance (vv. 4-6). When confronted by the stern fact of death, not everybody dives into an escape hatch and shouts, "Let's eat, drink, and be merry, for tomorrrow we die!" Many people just grit their teeth, square their shoulders and endure. They hold on to that ancient motto, "Where there's life, there's hope!" (That's a good paraphrase of v. 4.)

That motto goes as far back as the third century B.C. It's part of a conversation between two farmers who are featured in a poem by the Greek poet Theokritos. "Console yourself, dear Battos," says Korydon. "Things may be better tomorrow. While there's life there's hope. Only the dead have none." Shades of Ecclesiastes!

Solomon would be the last person to discourage anybody from hoping for the best. Better to be a living dog (and dogs were despised in that day) than a dead lion. All that the Preacher asked was that we have some common sense along with our hope, lest too late we find ourselves grasping a false hope.

To begin with, let's keep in mind that one day we shall die (v. 5). The Christian believer has "a living hope," not a "dead" hope, because the Saviour is alive and has conquered death (1 Peter 1:3-5; 2 Tim. 1:10). A hope that can be destroyed by death is a false hope and must be abandoned.

What Solomon wrote about the dead can be "reversed" and applied to the living. The dead do not know what is happening on earth, but the living know and can respond to it. The dead cannot add anything to their reward or their reputation, but the living can. The dead cannot relate to people on earth by loving, hating, or envying, but the living can. Solomon was emphasizing the importance of seizing opportunities while we live, rather than blindly hoping for something better in the future, because death will end our opportunities on this earth.

"The human body experiences a powerful gravitational pull in the direction of hope," wrote journalist Norman Cousins, who himself survived a near-fatal illness and a massive heart attack. "That is why the patient's hopes are the physician's secret weapon. They are the hidden ingredients in any prescription."

We endure because we hope, but "hope in hope" (like "faith in faith") is too often only a kind of self-hypnosis that keeps us from facing life honestly. While a patient may be better off with an optimistic attitude, it is dangerous for him to follow a *false hope* that may keep him from preparing for death. That kind of hope is hopeless. When the end comes, the patient's *outlook* may be cheerful, but the *outcome* will be tragic.

Life is not easy, but there is more to life than simply enduring. There is a third response to the fact of death, a response that can be made only by those who have trusted Jesus Christ as their Saviour.

Enjoyment (vv. 7-10). This has been one of Solomon's recurring themes (2:24; 3:12-15, 22; 5:18-20; 8:15), and he will bring it up again (11:9-10). His admonition "Go thy way!" means: "Don't sit around and brood! Get up and live!" Yes, death is coming, but God gives us good gifts to enjoy so enjoy them!

Solomon didn't urge us to join the "jet set" and start searching for exotic pleasures in far away places. Instead, he listed some of the common experiences of home life: happy leisurely meals (v. 7), joyful family celebrations (v. 8), a faithful, loving marriage (v. 9), and hard work (v. 10). What a contrast to modern society's formula for happiness: fast food and a full schedule, the addictive pursuit of everything new, "live-in marriages," and shortcuts guaranteed to help you avoid work but still get rich quick.

In recent years, many voices have united to call us back to the traditional values of life. Some people are getting tired of the emptiness of living on substitutes. They want something more substantial than the "right" labels on their clothes and the "right" names to drop at the "right" places. Like the younger brother in our Lord's parable (Luke 15:11-24), they have discovered that everything that's really important is back home at the Father's house.

Enjoy your meals (v. 7). The average Jewish family began the day with an early snack and then had a light meal ("brunch") sometime between 10:00 and noon. They didn't eat together again until after sunset. When their work was done they gathered for the main meal of the day. It consisted largely of bread and wine, perhaps milk and cheese, with a few vegetables and fruit in season, and sometimes fish. Meat was expensive and was served only on special occasions. It was a simple meal that was designed to nourish both the body and the soul, for eating together ("breaking bread") was a communal act of friendship and commitment.

King Solomon sat down to a daily feast (1 Kings 4:22-23), but there is evidence that he didn't always enjoy it. "Better a meal of vegetables where there is love than a fattened calf with hatred" (Prov. 15:17, NIV). "Better a dry crust with peace and quiet than a house full of feasting, with strife" (Prov. 17:1, NIV). The most important thing on any menu is *family love,* for love turns an ordinary meal into a banquet. When the children would rather eat at a friend's house than bring their friends home to enjoy their mother's cooking, it's time to take inventory of what goes on around the table.

Enjoy every occasion (v. 8). Life was difficult in the average home, but every family knew how to enjoy special occasions such as weddings and reunions. That's when they wore their white garments (a symbol of joy) and anointed themselves with expensive perfumes instead of the usual olive oil. These occasions were few, so everybody made the most of them.

But Solomon advised the people to wear white garments *always* and to anoint themselves *always* with special perfume. Of course, his congregation didn't take his words literally, because they knew what he was saying: make every occasion a special occasion, even if it's ordinary or routine. We must not express our thanksgiving and joy only when we are celebrating special events. "Rejoice in the Lord always. Again I will say, rejoice!" (Phil. 4:4, NKJV).

Among other things, this may be what Jesus had in mind when He told His disciples to become like little children (Matt. 18:1-6). An unspoiled child delights in the simple activities of life, even the routine activities, while a pampered child must be entertained by a variety of expensive amusements. It's not by searching for special things that we find joy, but by making the everyday things special.

Enjoy your marriage (v. 9). Solomon knew nothing about "live-in couples" or "trial marriages." He saw a wife as a gift from God (Prov. 18:22; 19:14) and marriage as a loving commitment that lasts a lifetime. No matter how difficult life may be, there is great joy in the home of the man and woman who love each other and are faithful to their marriage vows. Solomon would agree with psychiatrist M. Scott Peck who calls *commitment* "the foundation, the bedrock of any genuinely loving relationship" (*The Road Less Traveled,* p. 140).

It's too bad Solomon didn't live up to his own ideals. He forsook God's pattern for marriage and then allowed his many wives to seduce him from the Lord (1 Kings 11:1-8). If he wrote Ecclesiastes later in life, as I believe he did, then verse

9 is his confession, "Now I know better!"

Enjoy your work (v. 10). The Jewish people looked upon work, not as a curse, but as a stewardship from God. Even their rabbis learned a trade (Paul was a tent maker) and reminded them, "He who does not teach a son to work, teaches him to steal." Paul wrote, "If any would not work, neither should he eat" (2 Thes. 3:10).

"Do it with all your might" (NASB) suggests two things: Do your very best, and do it while you still have strength. The day may come when you will have to lay down your tools and make way for a younger and stronger worker. Colossians 3:17 applies this principle to the New Testament Christian.

The things that make up employment in this life will not be present in the grave (sheol, the realm of the dead), so make the most of your opportunities now. One day our works will be judged, and we want to receive a reward for His glory (1 Cor. 3:10ff; Col. 3:23-25).

If we fear God and walk by faith we will not try to escape or merely endure life. We will enjoy life and receive it happily as a gift from the Lord.

2. Life is unpredictable (Ecc. 9:11-18)

Anticipating the response of his listeners (and his readers), Solomon turned from his discussion of death and began to discuss life. "If death is unavoidable," somebody would argue, "then the smartest thing we can do is major on our strengths and concentrate on life. When death comes, at least we'll have the satisfaction of knowing we worked hard and achieved some success."

"Don't be too sure of that!" was Solomon's reply. "You can't guarantee what will happen in life, because life is unpredictable."

To begin with, our *abilities* are no guarantee of success (vv. 11-12). While it is generally true that the fastest runners win the races, the strongest soldiers win the battles, and the smartest and most skillful workers win the best jobs, it is also true that these same gifted people can fail miserably because of factors out of their control. The successful person knows how to make the most of "time and procedure" (8:5), but only the Lord can control "time and chance" (v. 11).

Solomon already affirmed that God has a time for everything (3:1-8), a purpose to be fulfilled in that time (8:6), and "something beautiful" to come out of it in the end (3:11). The word "chance" simply means occurrence or event. It has nothing to do with gambling. We might say, "I just happened to be in the right place at the right time, and I got the job. Ability had very little to do with it!"

Of course, Christians don't depend on such things as "luck" or "chance," because their confidence is in the loving providence of God. A dedicated Christian doesn't carry a rabbit's foot or trust in lucky days or numbers. Canadian humorist Stephen Leacock said, "I'm a great believer in luck. I find that the harder I work, the more I have of it." Christians trust God to guide them and help them in making decisions, and they believe that His will is best. They leave "time and chance" in His capable hands.

Who knows when trouble will arrive on the scene and wreck all our great plans (v. 12)? When they least expect it, fish are caught in the net and birds are caught in the trap. So men are snared in "evil times," sudden events that are beyond their control. That's why we should take to heart the admonition against boasting (James 4:13-17).

Second, our *opportunities* are no guarantee of success (vv. 13-18). It is not clear whether the wise man actually delivered the city, or whether he could have saved it, and was asked but did not heed. I lean toward the second explanation because it fits in better with verses 16-18. (The Hebrew allows for the translation "could have"; see the verse 15 footnote in the

NASB). The little city was besieged and the wise man could have delivered it, but nobody paid any attention to him. Verse 17 suggests that a ruler with a loud mouth got all of the attention and led the people into defeat. The wise man spoke quietly and was ignored. He had the opportunity for greatness but was frustrated by one loud ignorant man.

"One sinner [the loud ruler] destroys much good" (v. 18, NKJV) is a truth that is illustrated throughout the whole of Scripture, starting with Adam and his disobedience to God (Gen. 3; Rom. 5). Achan sinned and brought defeat on the army of Israel (Joshua 7). David's sin brought trouble to Israel (2 Sam. 24), and the revolt of Absalom led the nation into a civil war (2 Sam. 15ff).

Since death is unavoidable and life is unpredictable, the only course we can safely take is to yield ourselves into the hands of God and walk by faith in His Word. We don't live by explanations; we live by promises. We don't depend on luck but on the providential working of our loving Father as we trust His promises and obey His will.

As we walk by faith, we need not fear our "last enemy," because Jesus Christ has conquered death. "Fear not; I am the first and the last; I am He that liveth, and was dead; and, behold, I am alive for evermore" (Rev. 1:17-18). Because He is alive, and we live in Him, we don't look at life and say, "Vanity of vanities, all is vanity!"

Instead, we echo the confidence expressed by the Apostle Paul: "But thanks be to God, who gives us the victory through our Lord Jesus Christ. Therefore, my beloved brethren, be steadfast, immovable, always abounding in the work of the Lord, knowing that your labor is not in vain in the Lord" (1 Cor. 15:57-58, NKJV).

A Little Folly Is Dangerous

Before he concluded his message, Solomon thought it wise to remind his congregation once again of the importance of wisdom and the danger of folly. (The word "folly" is used nine times in this chapter.) In verse 1, he laid down the basic principle that folly creates problems for those who commit it. He had already compared a good name to fragrant perfume (7:1), so he used the image again. What dead flies are to perfume, folly is to the reputation of the wise person. The conclusion is logical: Wise people will stay away from folly!

Why is one person foolish and another wise? It all depends on the inclinations of the heart (v. 2). Solomon was not referring to the physical organ in the body, because everybody's heart is in the same place, except for those who might have some birth defect. Furthermore, the physical organ has nothing to do with wisdom or folly. Solomon was referring to the center of one's life, the "master control" within us that governs "the issues of life" (Prov. 4:23).

In the ancient world, the right hand was the place of power and honor, while the left hand represented weakness and rejection (Matt. 25:33, 41). Many people considered the left side to be "unlucky." (The English word "sinister" comes from a

Latin word that means "on the left hand.") Since the fool doesn't have wisdom in his heart, he gravitates toward that which is wrong (the left) and gets into trouble (see 2:14). People try to correct him, but he refuses to listen, and this tells everybody that he is a fool (v. 3).

Having laid down the principle, Solomon then applied it to four different "fools."

1. The foolish ruler (Ecc. 10:4-7)
If there is one person who needs wisdom, it is the ruler of a nation. When God asked Solomon what gift he especially wanted, the king asked for wisdom (1 Kings 3:3-28). Lyndon B. Johnson said, "A president's hardest task is not to *do* what's right, but to *know* what's right." That requires wisdom.

If a ruler is *proud,* he may say and do foolish things that cause him to lose the respect of his associates (v. 4). The picture here is of a proud ruler who easily becomes angry and takes out his anger on the attendants around him. Of course, if a man has no control over himself, how can he hope to have control over his people? "He who is slow to anger is better than the mighty and he who rules his spirit than he who takes a city" (Prov. 16:32, NKJV). "Whoever has no rule over his own spirit is like a city broken down, without walls" (Prov. 25:28, NKJV).

However, it isn't necessary for his servants to act like fools! In fact, that's the worse thing they can do (8:3). Far better that they control themselves, stay right where they are and seek to bring peace. "Through patience a ruler can be persuaded, and a gentle tongue can break a bone" (Prov. 25:15, NIV). "A king's wrath is a messenger of death, but a wise man will appease it" (Prov. 16:14, NIV).

To be sure, there is a righteous anger that sometimes needs to be displayed (Eph. 4:26), but not everything we call "righteous indignation" is really "righteous." It is so easy to give vent to jealousy and malice by disguising them as holy zeal for God. Not every religious crusader is motivated by love for God or obedience to the Word. His or her zeal could be a mask that is covering hidden anger or jealousy.

But if a ruler is too *pliable,* he is also a fool (vv. 5-7). If he lacks character and courage, he will put fools in the high offices and qualified people in the low offices. The servants will ride on horses while the noblemen will walk (see Prov. 19:10 and 30:21-22). If a ruler has incompetent people advising him, he is almost certain to govern the nation unwisely.

Solomon's son Rehoboam was proud and unyielding, and this led to the division of the kingdom (1 Kings 12:1-24). Instead of following the advice of the wise counselors, he listened to his youthful friends. He made the elders walk and he put the young men on the horses. On the other hand, more than one king in Jewish history has been so pliable that he turned out to be nothing but a figurehead. The best rulers (and leaders) are men and women who are tough-minded but tenderhearted, who put the best people on the horses and don't apologize for it.

2. Foolish workers (Ecc. 10:8-11)

Students are not agreed on what Solomon's point is in this graphic section. Was he saying that every job has its occupational hazards? If so, what lesson was he teaching, and why did he take so much space to illustrate the obvious? His theme is *folly,* and he certainly was not teaching that hard work is foolish because you might get injured! Throughout the book, Solomon emphasized the importance of honest labor and the joys it can bring. Why would he contradict that message?

I believe Solomon was describing people who attempted to do their work and suffered *because they were foolish.* One man dug a pit, perhaps a well or a place for storing grain, but fell into the pit himself. Why? Because he lacked wisdom and failed to take proper precautions. Frequently Scripture uses this as a picture of just retribution, but that doesn't seem to be the lesson here. (See Ps. 7:15; 9:15-16; 10:2; 35:8; 57:6; Prov. 26:27; 28:10.)

Another man broke through a hedge [wall, fence], perhaps while remodeling his house, and a serpent bit him. Serpents often found their way into hidden crevices and corners, and the man should have been more careful. He was overconfident and did not look ahead.

Verse 9 takes us to the quarries and the forests, where careless workers are injured cutting stones and splitting logs. Verse 10 pictures a foolish worker *par excellence:* a man who tried to split wood with a dull ax. The wise worker will pause in his labors and sharpen it. As the popular slogan says, "Don't work harder—work smarter!"

Snake charmers were common as entertainers in that day (v. 11, and see Ps. 58:4-5 and Jer. 8:17). Snakes have no external ears; they pick up sound waves primarily through the bone structure of the head. More than the music played by the charmer, it is the man's disciplined actions (swaying and "staring") that hold the snake's attention and keep the serpent under control. It is indeed an art.

Solomon described a performer who was bitten by the snake before the man had opportunity to "charm" it. Beside risking his life, the charmer could not collect any money from the spectators (see v. 11, NIV). They would only laugh at him. He was a fool because he rushed and acted as though the snake were charmed. He wanted to collect his money in a hurry and move to another location. The more "shows" he put on, the bigger his income. Instead, he made no money at all.

Some charmers had a mongoose available that "caught" the snake just at the right time and "saved" the man from being bitten. If for some reason the mongoose missed his cue, the serpent might attack the charmer, and that would be the end of the show. Either way, the man was foolish.

The common denominator among these "foolish workers" seems to be presumption. They were overconfident and ended up either hurting themselves or making their job harder.

3. Foolish talkers (Ecc. 10:12-15)

In the Book of Proverbs, Solomon had much to say about the speech of fools. In this paragraph, he pointed out four characteristics of their words.

First, they are *destructive* words (v. 12). The wise person will speak gracious words that are suited to the listeners and the occasion (Prov. 10:32; 25:11). Whether in personal conversation or public ministry, our Lord always knew the right thing to say at the right time (Isa. 50:4). We should try to emulate Him. But the fool blurts out whatever is on his mind and doesn't stop to consider who might be hurt by it. In the end, it is the fool himself who is hurt the most: "a fool is consumed by his own lips" (Ecc. 10:12, NIV).

In Scripture, destructive words are compared to weapons of war (Prov. 25:18), a fire (James 3:5-6), and a poisonous beast (James 3:7-8). We may try to hurt others with our lies, slander, and angry words, but we are really hurting ourselves the most. "He who guards his mouth preserves his life, but he who opens wide his lips shall have destruction" (Prov. 13:3, NKJV). "Whoever guards his mouth and tongue keeps his soul from troubles" (Prov. 21:23, NKJV).

They are also *unreasonable* words (v. 13). What he says doesn't make sense. And the longer he talks, the crazier it becomes. "The beginning of his talking is folly, and the end of it is wicked madness" (NASB). He would be better off to keep quiet, because all that he says only lets everybody know that he is a fool (5:3). Paul called these people "unruly and vain talkers" (Titus 1:10), which J.B. Phillips translates "who will not recognize authority, who talk nonsense" (PH).

Occasionally in my travels, I meet people who will talk about anything anybody brings up, as though they were the greatest living experts on that subject. When the Bible or religion comes into the conversation, I quietly wait for them to hang themselves; and they rarely disappoint me. The Jewish writer Shalom Aleichem said, "You can tell when a fool speaks: he grinds much and produces little."

Third, they are *uncontrolled* words (v. 14a). The fool is "full of words" without realizing that he is saying nothing. "In the multitude of words, sin is not lacking, but he who restrains his lips is wise" (Prov. 10:19, NKJV). The person who can control his or her tongue is able to discipline the entire body (James 3:1-2). Jesus said, "But let your 'Yes' be 'Yes' and your 'No' be 'No.' For whatever is more than this is from the evil one" (Matt. 5:37, NKJV).

Finally, they are *boastful* words (14b-15). Foolish people talk about the future as though they either know all about it or are in control of what will happen. "Do not boast about tomorrow, for you do not know what a day may bring forth" (Prov. 27:1, NKJV). Several times before, Solomon has emphasized man's ignorance of the future (3:22; 6:12; 8:7; 9:12), a truth that wise people receive but fools reject. (See James 4:13-17.)

There is a bit of humor here. The fool boasts about his future plans and wearies people with his talk, but he can't even find the way to the city. In Bible times, the roads to the cities were well-marked so that any traveler could find his way, but the fool is so busy talking about the future that he loses his way in the present. "He can't find his way to the city" was probably an ancient proverb about stupidity, not unlike our "He's so dumb, he couldn't learn the route to run an elevator."

4. Foolish officers (Ecc. 10:16-20)

Solomon has already described foolish rulers. Now he exposes the folly of the officers who work under those rulers, the bureaucrats who were a part of the machinery of the kingdom. He gave four characteristics of these foolish men.

Indulgence (vv. 16-17). If the king is immature, the people he gathers around him will reflect that immaturity and take advantage of it. But if he is a true nobleman, he will surround himself with noble officers who will put the good of the country first. Real leaders use their authority to build the nation, while mere officeholders use the nation to build their authority. They use public funds for their own selfish purposes, throwing parties and having a good time.

It is a judgment of God when a people are given immature leaders (Isa. 3:1-5). This can happen to a nation or to a local church. The term "elder" (Titus 1:5ff) implies maturity and experience in the Christian life, and it is wrong for a believer to be thrust into leadership too soon (1 Tim. 3:6). Age is no guarantee of maturity (1 Cor. 3:1-4; Heb. 5:11-14), and youth sometimes outstrips its elders in spiritual zeal. Oswald Chambers said, "Spiritual maturity is not reached by the passing of the years, but by obedience to the will of God." The important thing is maturity, not just age.

The *New International Version* translates verse 16, "Woe to you, O land whose king was a servant." The suggestion is that this servant became king with the help of his friends (cf. 4:13-14). Now he was obligated to give them all jobs so he could remain on the throne. In spite of their selfish and expensive indulgence, these hirelings could not be dismissed, because the king's security depended on them. To the victor belong the spoils!

Incompetence (v. 18). These foolish officers are so busy with enjoyment that they have no time for employment, and both the buildings and the organization start to fall apart. "He also who is slothful in his work is brother to him that is a great waster" (Prov. 18:9). There is a difference between those who *use* an office and those who merely *hold* an office (1 Tim.

3:10). Immature people enjoy the privileges and ignore the responsibilities, while mature people see the responsibilities as privileges and use them to help others.

Woodrow Wilson wrote, "A friend of mine says that every man who takes office in Washington either grows or swells; when I give a man an office, I watch him carefully to see whether he is swelling or growing."

Indifference (v. 19). This verse declares the personal philosophy of the foolish officers: Eat all you can, enjoy all you can, and get all you can. They are totally indifferent to the responsibilities of their office or the needs of the people. In recent years, various developing nations have seen how easy it is for unscrupulous leaders to steal government funds in order to build their own kingdoms. Unfortunately, it has also happened recently to some religious organizations.

"For the love of money is a root of all kinds of evil" (1 Tim. 6:10, NKJV). The prophet Amos cried out against the wicked rulers of his day who trampled on the heads of the poor and treated them like the dust of the earth (Amos 2:7, and see 4:1; 5:11-12). The courts might not catch up with all the unscrupulous politicians, but God will eventually judge them, and His judgment will be just.

Indiscretion (v. 20). The familiar saying "A little bird told me" probably originated from this verse. You can imagine a group of these officers having a party in one of their private rooms and, instead of toasting the king, they are cursing ["making light of"] him. Of course, they wouldn't do this if any of the king's friends were present, but they were sure that the company would faithfully keep the secret. Alas, somebody told the king what was said, and this gave him reason to punish them or dismiss them from their offices.

Even if we can't respect the person in the office, we must respect the office (Rom. 13:1-7; 1 Peter 2:13-17). "You shall not revile God, nor curse a ruler of your people" (Ex. 22:28).

These hirelings were certainly indiscreet when they cursed the king, for they should have known that one of their number would use this event either to intimidate his friends or to ingratiate himself with the ruler. A statesman asks, "What is best for my country?" A politician asks, "What is best for my party?" But a mere officeholder, a hireling, asks, "What is safest and most profitable for me?"

This completes Solomon's review of his fourth argument that life is not worth living, "the certainty of death" (2:12-23). He has concluded that life is indeed worth living, even though death is unavoidable (9:1-10) and life is unpredictable (9:11-18). What we must do is avoid folly (ch. 10) and live by the wisdom of God.

This also concludes the second part of his discourse. He has reviewed the four arguments presented in chapters 1 and 2, and has decided that life was really worth living after all. The best thing we can do is to trust God, do our work, accept what God sends us, and enjoy each day of our lives to the glory of God (3:12-15, 22; 5:18-20; 8:15; 9:7-10). All that remains for the Preacher is to conclude his discourse with a practical application and this he does in chapters 11 and 12. He will bring together all the various strands of truth that he has woven into his sermon, and he will show us what God expects us to do if we are to be satisfied.

TWELVE

What Life Is All About

I s life worth living?"
That was the question the Preacher raised when he began
the discourse that we call Ecclesiastes. After experimenting
and investigating "life under the sun," he concluded, "No, life
is *not* worth living!" He gave four arguments to support his
conclusion: the monotony of life, the vanity of wisdom, the
futility of wealth, and the certainty of death.

Being a wise man, Solomon reviewed his arguments and this
time brought God into the picture. What a difference it made.
He realized that life was not monotonous but filled with chal-
lenging situations from God, each in its own time and each for
its own purpose. He also learned that wealth could be enjoyed
and employed to the glory of God. Though man's wisdom
couldn't explain everything, Solomon concluded that it was
better to follow God's wisdom than to practice man's folly. As
for the certainty of death, there is no way to escape it; and it
ought to motivate us to enjoy life now and make the most of
the opportunities God gives us.

Now Solomon was ready for his conclusion and personal
application. What he did was present *four pictures of life* and
attach to each picture a practical admonition for his listeners

(and readers) to heed. The development looks like this:

Life is an ADVENTURE—live by faith (11:1-6)
Life is a GIFT—enjoy it (11:7–12:8)
Life is a SCHOOL—learn your lessons (12:9-12)
Life is a STEWARDSHIP—fear God (12:13-14)

These four pictures parallel the four arguments that Solomon had wrestled with throughout the book. Life is not monotonous; rather, it is an adventure of faith that is anything but predictable or tedious. Yes, death is certain, but life is a gift from God and He wants us to enjoy it. Are there questions we can't answer and problems we can't solve? Don't despair. God teaches us His truth as we advance in "the school of life," and He will give us wisdom enough to make sensible decisions. Finally, as far as wealth is concerned, all of life is a stewardship from God; and one day He will call us to give an account. Therefore, "fear God, and keep His commandments" (12:13).

1. Life is an adventure: live by faith (Ecc. 11:1-6)
When I was a boy, I practically lived in the public library during the summer months. I loved books, the building was cool, and the librarians gave me the run of the place since I was one of their best customers. One summer I read nothing but true adventure stories written by real heroes like Frank Buck and Martin Johnson. These men knew the African jungles better than I knew my hometown! I was fascinated by *I Married Adventure,* the autobiography of Martin Johnson's wife Osa. When Clyde Beatty brought his circus to town, I was in the front row watching him "tame" the lions.

Since those boyhood days, life has become a lot calmer for me, but I trust I haven't lost that sense of adventure.

In fact, as I get older, I'm asking God to keep me from getting set in my ways in a life that is routine, boring, and predictable. "I don't want my life to end in a swamp," said British expositor F.B. Meyer. I agree with him. When I trusted Jesus Christ as my Saviour, "I married adventure"; and that meant living by faith and expecting the unexpected.

Solomon used two activities to illustrate his point: the merchant sending out his ships (vv. 1-2) and the farmer sowing his seed (vv. 3-6). In both activities, a great deal of faith is required, because neither the merchant nor the farmer can control the circumstances. The ships might hit a reef, meet a storm, or be attacked by pirates and the cargo lost. Bad weather, blight, or insects might destroy the crop, and the farmer's labor would be in vain. However, if the merchant and the farmer waited until the circumstances were ideal, they would never get anything done! Life has a certain amount of risk to it, and that's where faith comes in.

The merchant (vv. 1-2). "Cast thy bread upon the waters" may be paraphrased, "Send out your grain in ships." Solomon himself was involved in various kinds of trade, so it was natural for him to use this illustration (1 Kings 10:15, 22). It would be months before the ships would return with their precious cargo; but when they did, the merchant's faith and patience would be rewarded. Verse 2 suggests that he spread out his wealth and not put everything into one venture. After all, true faith is not presumption.

"For you do not know" is a key phrase in this section (vv. 2, 5, 6). Man is ignorant of the future, but he must not allow his ignorance to make him so fearful that he becomes either careless or paralyzed. On the contrary, not knowing the future should make us more careful in what we plan and what we do. Verse 2 can be interpreted, "Send cargo on seven or eight ships, because some of them are bound to bring back a good return on the investment." In other words, "Don't put all your eggs in one basket."

The farmer (vv. 3-6). Daniel Webster called farmers "the

founders of civilization," and Thomas Jefferson said they were "the chosen people of God." Farming has never been easy work, and this was especially true in the Holy Land in Bible days. The Jews tilled a rocky soil, and they depended on the early and latter rains to nourish their seed. Nobody can predict the weather, let alone control it, and the farmer is at the mercy of nature.

Verse 3 contrasts the clouds with the tree. Clouds are always changing. They come and go, and the farmer hopes they will spill their precious water on his fields. Trees are somewhat permanent. They stand in the same place, unless a storm topples them; and then they lie there and rot. The past [the tree] cannot be changed, but the present [the clouds] is available to us, and we must seize each opportunity.

But don't sit around waiting for ideal circumstances (v. 4). The wind is never right for the sower and the clouds are never right for the reaper. If you are looking for an excuse for doing nothing, you can find one. Billy Sunday said that an excuse was "the skin of a reason stuffed with a lie." Life is an adventure and often we must launch out by faith, even when the circumstances seem adverse.

Just as nobody knows "the way of the wind" (v. 5, NKJV, and see John 3:8) or how the fetus is formed in the womb (Ps. 139:14-15), so nobody knows the works of God in His creation. God has a time and a purpose for everything (3:1-11), and we must live by faith in His Word. Therefore, use each day wisely (v. 6). Get up early and sow your seed, and work hard until evening. Do the job at hand and "redeem the time" (Eph. 5:15-17), trusting God to bless at least some of the tasks you have accomplished. Just as the merchant sends out more than one ship, so the farmer works more than one crop.

Life is an adventure of faith, and each of us is like a merchant, investing today in that which will pay dividends tomorrow. We are like the farmer, sowing various kinds of seeds in different soils, trusting God for the harvest (Gal. 6:8-9; Ps. 126:5-6; Hos. 10:12). If we worried about the wind toppling a tree over on us, or the clouds drenching us with rain, we would never accomplish anything. "Of course, there is no formula for success," said famous concert pianist Arthur Rubinstein, "except perhaps an unconditional acceptance of life and what it brings."

2. Life is a gift: enjoy it (Ecc. 11:7–12:8)

This is Solomon's sixth and final admonition that we accept life as a gift and learn to enjoy all that God shares with us (see 2:24; 3:12-15, 22; 5:18-20; 8:15; 9:7-10). In order to do this, we must obey three instructions: rejoice (11:7-9), remove (11:10), and remember (12:1-8).

Rejoice (11:7-9). What a joy it is to anticipate each new day and accept it as a fresh gift from God! I confess that I never realized what it meant to live a day at a time until I was nearly killed in an auto accident back in 1966. It was caused by a drunk driver careening around a curve at between 80 and 90 miles per hour. By the grace of God, I had no serious injuries; but my stay in the Intensive Care Ward, and my time of recuperation at home, made me a firm believer in Deut. 33:25, "As thy days, so shall thy strength be." Now when I awaken early each morning, I thank God for the new day; and I ask Him to help me use it wisely for His glory and to enjoy it as His gift.

Solomon especially instructed the young people to take advantage of the days of youth before the "days of darkness" would arrive. He was not suggesting that young people have no problems or that older people have no joys. He was simply making a generalization that youth is the time for enjoyment, before the problems of old age start to reveal themselves.

My middle name is Wendell; I'm named after Wendell P. Loveless, who was associated for many years with the Moody

Bible Institute in Chicago, especially radio station WMBI. He lived into his nineties and was alert to the very end. During one of our visits with him, he told me and my wife, "I don't go out much now because my parents won't let me—Mother Nature and Father Time!"

Young people have to watch their hearts and their eyes, because either or both can lead them into sin (Num. 15:39; Prov. 4:23; Matt. 5:27-30). "Walk in the ways of your heart" (NKJV) is not an encouragement to go on a youthful fling and satisfy the sinful desires within (Jer. 17:9; Mark 7:20-23). It is rather a reminder for young people to enjoy the special pleasures that belong to youth and can never be experienced again in quite the same way. Those of us who are older need to remember that God expects young people to act like young people. The tragedy is that too many older people are trying to act like young people!

Solomon's warning is evidence that he doesn't have sinful pleasures in mind: "God will bring you into judgment."

God does give us "all things richly to enjoy" (1 Tim. 6:17), but it is always wrong to enjoy the pleasures of sin. The young person who enjoys life in the will of God will have nothing to worry about when the Lord returns.

Remove (v. 10). Privileges must be balanced by personal responsibilities. Young people must put anxiety out of their hearts (Matt. 6:24-34) and evil away from their flesh (2 Cor. 7:1). The word translated "sorrow" means "vexation, inner pain, anxiety." If we are living in the will of God, we will have the peace of God in our hearts (Phil. 4:6-9). The sins of the flesh only destroy the body and can bring eternal judgment to the soul.

The phrase "childhood and youth are vanity" does not mean that these stages in life are unimportant and a waste of time. Quite the opposite is true! The best way to have a happy adult life and a contented old age is to get a good start early in life and avoid the things that will bring trouble later on. Young people who take care of their minds and bodies, avoid the destructive sins of the flesh, and build good habits of health and holiness, have a better chance for happy adult years than those who "sow their wild oats" and pray for a crop failure.

The phrase means "childhood and youth are transient." These precious years go by so quickly, and we must not waste our opportunities for preparing for the future. The Hebrew word translated "youth" can mean "the dawning" or "blackness of hair" (as opposed to gray hair). Youth is indeed the time of "dawning"; and before we know it, the sun will start to set. Therefore, make the most of those "dawning years," because you will never see them again. "Youthful sins lay a foundation for aged sorrows," said Charles Spurgeon; and he was right.

Remember (12:1-8). This third instruction means more than "think about God." It means "pay attention to, consider with the intention of obeying." It is Solomon's version of Matthew 6:33, "But seek first the kingdom of God and His righteousness" (NKJV). How easy it is to neglect the Lord when you are caught up in the enjoyments and opportunities of youth. We know that dark days (11:8) and difficult [evil] days (12:1) are coming, so we had better lay a good spiritual foundation as early in life as possible. During our youthful years, the sky is bright (11:7); but the time will come when there will be darkness and one storm after another.

Verses 3-7 give us one of the most imaginative descriptions of old age and death found anywhere in literature. Students don't agree on all the details of interpretation, but most of them do see here a picture of a house that is falling apart and finally turns to dust. A dwelling place is one biblical metaphor for the human body (Job 4:19; 2 Cor. 5:1-2 [a tent]; 2 Peter 1:13 [a tent]), and taking down a house or tent is a picture of death. The meaning may be:

keepers of the house—Your arms and hands tremble.

strong men—Your legs, knees, and shoulders weaken and you walk bent over.

grinders—You start to lose your teeth.

windows—Your vision begins to deteriorate.

doors—Either your hearing starts to fail, or you close your mouth because you've lost your teeth.

grinding—You can't chew your food, or your ears can't pick up the sounds outdoors.

rise up—You wake up with the birds early each morning, and wish you could sleep longer.

music—Your voice starts to quaver and weaken.

afraid—You are terrified of heights and afraid of falling while you walk down the street.

almond tree—If you have any hair left, it turns white, like almond blossoms.

grasshopper—You just drag yourself along, like a grasshopper at the close of the summer season.

desire—You lose your appetite, or perhaps your sexual desire.

long home—You go to your eternal [long] home and people mourn your death.

Verse 6 describes a golden bowl—a lamp—hanging from the ceiling on a silver chain. The chain breaks and the bowl breaks. The fragile "cord of life" is snapped and the light of life goes out. Only wealthy people could have such costly lamps, so Solomon may be hinting that death is no respecter of persons.

The verse also pictures a well with a windlass for bringing up a pitcher filled with water. One day the wheel breaks, the pitcher is shattered, and the end comes. The fountain of water was an ancient image for life (Ps. 36:8-9; Rev. 21:6). When the machinery of life stops working, the water of life stops flowing. The heart stops pumping, the blood stops circulating, and death has come. The spirit leaves the body (James 2:26; Luke 23:46; Acts 7:59), the body begins to decay, and eventually it turns to dust.

For the last time in his discourse, the Preacher said, "Vanity of vanities . . . all is vanity." The book closes where it began (1:2), emphasizing the emptiness of life without God. When you look at life "under the sun," everything does seem vain; but when you know Jesus Christ as your Saviour, "your labor is not in vain in the Lord" (1 Cor. 15:58).

3. Life is a school: learn your lessons (Ecc. 12:9-12)
Someone has said that life is like a school, except that sometimes you don't know what the lessons are until you have failed the examination. God teaches us primarily from His Word; but He also teaches us through creation, history, and the various experiences of life. Solomon explained the characteristics of his own work as a teacher of God's truth.

To begin with, his teaching was *wise* (v. 9); for Solomon was the wisest of men (1 Kings 3:3-28). The king studied and explored many subjects, and some of his conclusions he wrote down in proverbs.

His teaching was also *orderly* (v. 9). After studying a matter, he weighed his conclusions carefully, and then arranged them in an orderly fashion. His whole approach was certainly scientific. We may not always see the pattern behind his arrangement, but it is there just the same.

Solomon sought to be *careful* in his teaching, so he used "acceptable words." This means "pleasing" or "gracious" words (10:12) that would win the attention of his listeners and readers. However, at no time did he dilute his message or flatter his congregation. He always used *upright words of truth*. (See Prov. 8:6-11.) Like our Lord Jesus Christ, the king was able to combine "grace and truth" (John 1:17; Luke 4:16-32).

The Preacher claimed that his words were *inspired,* given by God, the One Shepherd (v. 11). Inspiration was the special miracle ministry of the Holy Spirit that enabled men of God to write the Word of God as God wanted it written, complete and without error (2 Tim. 3:16-17; 2 Peter 1:20-21).

He compared his words to "goads" and "nails" (v. 11), both of which are necessary if people are to learn God's truth. The "goads" prod the people to pay attention and to pursue truth, while the "nails" give them something on which to hang what they have learned. Good teaching requires both: the students must be motivated to study and the instructors must be able to "nail things down" so that the lessons make sense.

On the surface, verse 12 seems to be a negative view of learning; but such is not the case. The statement is a warning to the student not to go beyond what God has written in His Word. Indeed, there are many books; and studying them can be a wearisome chore. But don't permit man's books to rob you of God's wisdom. "Be warned, my son, of anything in addition to them [the words of the wise]" (v. 12, NIV). These "nails" are sure and you can depend on them. Don't test God's truth by the "many books" written by men; test men's books by the truth of God's Word.

Yes, life is a school; and we must humble ourselves and learn all we can. Our textbook is the Bible, and the Holy Spirit is our Teacher (John 14:26; 15:26; 16:12-15). The Spirit can use gifted human teachers to instruct us, but He longs to teach us personally from His Word (Ps. 119:97-104). There are always new lessons to learn and new examinations to face as we seek to grow in grace and in the knowledge of our Saviour (2 Peter 3:18).

4. Life is a stewardship: fear God (Ecc. 12:13-14)
We don't own our lives, because life is the gift of God (Acts 17:24-28). We are stewards of our lives, and one day we must

134

give an account to God of what we have done with His gift. Some people are only spending their lives; others are wasting their lives; a few are investing their lives. Corrie ten Boom said, "The measure of a life, after all, is not its duration but its donation." If our lives are to count, we must fulfill three obligations.

Fear God (v. 13). Ecclesiastes ends where the Book of Proverbs begins (Prov. 1:7), with an admonition for us to fear the Lord. (See 3:14; 5:7; 7:18; and 8:12-13.) The "fear of the Lord" is that attitude of reverence and awe that His people show to Him because they love Him and respect His power and His greatness. The person who fears the Lord will pay attention to His Word and obey it. He or she will not tempt the Lord by deliberately disobeying or by "playing with sin." An unholy fear makes people run away from God, but a holy fear brings them to their knees in loving submission to God.

"The remarkable thing about fearing God," wrote Oswald Chambers, "is that, when you fear God, you fear nothing else; whereas, if you do not fear God, you fear everything else." The prophet Isaiah says it perfectly in Isaiah 8:13, and the psalmist describes such a man in Psalm 112.

Keep His commandments (v. 13). God created life and He alone knows how it should be managed. He wrote the "manual of instructions" and wise is the person who reads and obeys. "When all else fails, read the instructions!"

The fear of the Lord must result in obedient living, otherwise that "fear" is only a sham. The dedicated believer will want to spend time daily in Scripture, getting to know the Father better and discovering His will. "The fear of the Lord is the beginning of knowledge, but fools despise wisdom and instruction" (Prov. 1:7).

The last phrase in verse 13 can be translated "this is the end of man" (i.e., his purpose in life), or "this is for all men." Campbell Morgan suggests "this is the whole of man." He

135

writes in *The Unfolding Message of the Bible*, "Man, in his entirety, must begin with God; the whole of man, the fear of God" (p. 228). When Solomon looked at life "under the sun," everything was fragmented and he could see no pattern. But when he looked at life from God's point of view, everything came together into one whole. If man wants to have wholeness, he must begin with God.

Prepare for final judgment (v. 14). "God shall judge the righteous and the wicked" (3:17). "But know that for all these God will bring you into judgment" (11:9, NKJV). Man may seem to get away with sin (8:11), but their sins will eventually be exposed and judged righteously. Those who have not trusted the Lord Jesus Christ will be doomed forever.

"The eternity of punishment is a thought which crushes the heart," said Charles Spurgeon. "The Lord God is slow to anger, but when he is once aroused to it, as he will be against those who finally reject his Son, he will put forth all his omnipotence to crush his enemies."

Six times in his discourse, Solomon told us to enjoy life while we can; but at no time did he advise us to enjoy sin. The joys of the present depend on the security of the future. If you know Jesus Christ as your Saviour, then your sins have already been judged on the cross; and "there is therefore now no condemnation to them who are in Christ Jesus" (Rom. 8:1 and see John 5:24). But if you die having never trusted Christ, you will face judgment at His throne and be lost forever (Rev. 20:11-15).

Is life worth living? Yes, *if you are truly alive through faith in Jesus Christ.* Then you can be satisfied, no matter what God may permit to come to your life.

"He who has the Son has life; he who does not have the Son of God does not have life" (1 John 5:12, NKJV).

You can receive life in Christ and—*be satisfied!*